FAY'S FAMILY FOOD

For Dan, Parker and Sonny,
my family, my life

MICHAEL JOSEPH
Published by the Penguin Group
Penguin Books Ltd, 80 Strand, London WC2R 0RL, England
Penguin Group (USA) Inc., 375 Hudson Street, New York,
New York 10014, USA
Penguin Group (Canada), 90 Eglinton Avenue East, Suite 700,
Toronto, Ontario, Canada M4P 2Y3
(a division of Pearson Penguin Canada Inc.)
Penguin Ireland, 25 St Stephen's Green, Dublin 2, Ireland
(a division of Penguin Books Ltd)
Penguin Group (Australia), 250 Camberwell Road, Camberwell,
Victoria 3124, Australia (a division of Pearson Australia Group Pty Ltd)
Penguin Books India Pvt Ltd, 11 Community Centre,
Panchsheel Park, New Delhi – 110 017, India
Penguin Group (NZ), 67 Apollo Drive, Rosedale, North Shore 0632,
New Zealand (a division of Pearson New Zealand Ltd)
Penguin Books (South Africa) (Pty) Ltd, 24 Sturdee Avenue,
Rosebank, Johannesburg 2196, South Africa
Penguin Books Ltd, Registered Offices: 80 Strand,
London WC2R 0RL, England

www.penguin.com

First published 2009
5

Text copyright © Fay Ripley, 2009

Photography copyright © David Munns, 2009

The moral right of the author has been asserted

Printed in China

Colour reproduction by Altaimage Ltd

Set in Meta, Clarendon, Marshmallow World © Dani Foster Herring,
1999 and Wendy LP Std

A CIP catalogue record for this book is available from the British Library

ISBN: 978–0–718–15460–8

FAY RIPLEY

FAY'S FAMILY FOOD

Delicious recipes where one meal feeds everyone. Whatever age!

Photography by David Munns

MICHAEL JOSEPH
an imprint of
PENGUIN BOOKS

Contents

Introduction

It seems to me that our relationship with food changes according to our circumstances.

Here are mine . . .

Fay's food journey

First, I was the single woman about town. Grabbing food on the run or at work (*Cold Feet*: great show, food fit for your dog). With money to burn and time to indulge myself, eating out was the norm and not a treat.

Then came a boyfriend (Dan), and with him came cosy nights at home, cooking and pretending to be husband and wife. The longer we were together, the more we shared our love of all things edible.

Then, after I had cooked a particularly good lamb shank, he popped the question . . . 'Will you give me that recipe? . . . Oh, and will you cook for me for the rest of our lives?' (Or words to that effect.) On a sugar high from the raspberry soufflé, I said 'yes' to both. Very quickly, a small human started to grow inside my body (I still don't really understand how that happens). I stopped cooking and started to eat liquorice.

When our new baby flatmate arrived (a little girl called Parker), Dan took over the cooking (barbies played a big role; he's an Aussie). Whilst I was left feeling like an old overworked dairy cow, longing for the time my daughter would want something on the menu other than me . . .

When that moment came, I read every book on the market, watched videos, scoured the internet, all to discover the secret of producing 'a good eater' (not to be confused with an anteater). Finally I came to the conclusion that the best route through this maze of advice was to wean her on fresh, organic produce, varying the tastes as much as possible. Even at an early stage, I introduced her to loads of herbs, rye and spelt breads and wonderful tastes that made her little mouth open like a baby bird's.

And what do you know? It worked. She loves food (well, most of it). Luck or judgement? Not sure, but it does make sense, I guess.

Now, while I was busy turning my daughter into a foodie, I had totally neglected my own culinary needs. Dan's favourite lamb shanks were a thing of the past, as the last thing I wanted to do after preparing Parker's meal was to start on ours. Poor Dan, his dream of a 1940s domestic goddess was in pieces.

The next couple of years saw us working, travelling, moving and, just as Parker hit an age where we could all enjoy the same food at the same time, bang! Another human bun in my not-so-human-any-more oven (a baby boy, Sonny).

And that's when the real journey began. The realization that I wanted us to enjoy the same food and eat it together, where possible. It made sense for them and, more to the point, for me.

So I started working our meals out around all of us. Not separate ingredients, age dependent. For some reason, in this country, we have lost the ability to eat together. We all shout 'There's no time!', but it's a flawed argument. We have to eat, right? So eat something tasty. It doesn't have to take long, but at least you feel good afterwards. The other excuse we make to ourselves is that it's easier to just grab the same old thing or a packet of something bland, but I know so many people who hate shopping from their dull grocery list because they are not looking forward to cooking it. They are bored and can't think what to buy everyone for the week ahead. Monday: pizza for Parker, jars and some fishfingers for little Sonny, a takeaway for us. Well, meatballs for everyone sounds so much easier to me. Also, I reckon it's cheaper to all eat from the same proverbial pot. Live off the leftovers and the smiles that inevitably come your way after a good meal.

Look, the Italians do it. Why can't we? In fact, the whole of the EU seems to have clung on to their ancestral dining habits. So stop the clock and bung a chicken in the oven. It's time to eat, talk and be merry!

Food brings people together. I am not suggesting that a moist muffin turns a mad, dysfunctional family into the Von Trapps, but food makes us happy, healthy and ... full.

Reality check

Now, I get that none of us have any spare time. That money is a constant issue for most people. That not all kids eat well (or indeed anything). That pre-prepared jars seem easier and that doing it 'the cookbook way' seems frankly unrealistic.

But this book is meant to offer suggestions and inspiration. You don't have to do it every day. It's there to get you in the swing; to get organized, write lists and find fifteen minutes to knock something up that you are proud to see go into your kids' naughty little mouths.

Food as fun, not fuel. And here is the bonus: it can be delicious not only for them but for you, your family and your friends too. (For really impressive grown-up recipes, please feel free to use proper cookbooks from the big boys.)

The idea is to cook food from which you can remove your babies' and kids' portions if needs be, before adding the more challenging ingredients for yourselves; or better still, all tuck in together. One delicious meal for all of you.

I am living this. It's easy. I have kept it simple. Sometimes I get it wrong. Sometimes I have to throw pans away (multi-tasking can lead to burnt food). But it is always exciting to see my family and friends get stuck in to great grub that I have put together.

···

PS The other day someone asked Parker (five) what she wanted to be when she grew up. She replied, 'A chef.' The same question was put to Sonny (one). He replied, 'A truck.' I'm working on him.

'It seems to
me that our
relationship
with food
changes
according
to our
circumstances.'

A note about ingredients

Spelt is one of the first grains to have been grown by early farmers, as long ago as 5000 BC, and is now gaining popularity at an incredible speed as an alternative to the overprocessed, bleached flour used in so many products today. The grain is naturally high in fibre and contains significantly more protein than wheat. It is also higher in B-complex vitamins and both simple and complex carbohydrates. It has less gluten and is much easier on the digestive system.

I discovered spelt when, after a really bad bout of food poisoning, my doc told me to lay off the wheat so that my stomach could recover. Searching for an alternative, I came across spelt bread, which tasted great, and I have not looked back. I am wheat-intolerant but the rest of the family all love it too. So I tend to buy spelt pasta and bread for the kids as it is so much kinder to their stomachs, and I always bake with the flour. It behaves the same as normal flour, as I have indicated in the recipes. White spelt flour is like plain white flour and spelt flour is like wholemeal flour. There are more and more products available. You can already buy bread of all types, biscuits, cakes, pastas, croissants, cereals and more. I mainly have to go to wholefood shops or specialist stores, but some supermarkets are starting to supply it. So keep an eye on the shelves.

PS If you or the kids have tummy upsets of any kind, I would highly recommend keeping them off the wheat and all wheat products. Find some spelt if you can as it is so much gentler on the digestive system.

Salt is addictive. The more you have, the more you crave. I have kept salt out of all the recipes, adding it only on the plate as a personal preference. This is so that the kids don't get overloaded with the stuff. Very quickly you get used to this and often you just wouldn't miss it. Feel free to put it back in, but at least try it my way first.

Booze: I have also kept alcohol out of the recipes. I know it burns off, but it just doesn't feel right to marinate a chop in gin and serve it up to toddlers.

Freezing

Anything that I think freezes well I have indicated with a ❄. Defrost thoroughly before reheating.

BREAKFAST AT RIPLEY'S

I'm up at 5.45 a.m. with the first gurglings of the Lapaine/Ripley dawn chorus. Bottle (milk, not vodka) and breakfast need to be on the go. We have to wash, dress, feed the kids, husband, goldfish, and the soul if time permits. Nothing out of the ordinary, but nevertheless I am completely knackered by 9 a.m., just dreaming of the moment the day is over and I can sink back into my under-used bed.

Well, God knows I'm not going to produce a full English, but seeing everyone eating a proper, healthy breakfast, fuelling them all for the day ahead, makes me feel happy. Not as happy as a new handbag makes me feel, but happy.

Try not to get too stuck in a breakfast rut, which is easy to do. Even if it just means being a little more adventurous on weekends. Sunday is a great chance to all sit down around the same table at the same time, to pancakes or scrambled eggs.

It's so healthy to big it up at breakfast, tuck in at lunch and frankly by dinner it's every man for himself. Go on, think outside the cereal box…

Breakfast at Ripley's

Posh scrambled eggs on toast

Honey-sweetened breakfast muffins

Passionate cooked apples

All-American blueberry pancakes

Breakfast trifle

Parker's cheese on toast

Baked breakfast eggs

Good morning granola

Fruit kebabs

Posh scrambled eggs on toast

Yum! This is really tasty and apart from being a family favourite, it is easily good enough to serve as a lunch or light supper for friends.

ALL YOU NEED IS

8 slices of brioche bread

a small bunch of chives

5 large eggs, beaten

a knob of butter

125g packet smoked salmon

4 dessertspoons half-fat crème fraîche

4 teaspoons black lumpfish caviar

1 tablespoon capers

ALL YOU DO IS

1. Toast the brioche slices.

2. Snip the chives into the beaten eggs.

3. In a non-stick pan, melt the butter, then scramble the eggs on a low heat, until cooked but still moist. (They keep cooking, so take them off the heat before they dry out.)

4. Pile the egg on to the toast. Then lay on some salmon. Next, add a dessertspoon of crème fraîche, a teaspoon of caviar and finally a scattering of capers.

Serve with freshly squeezed orange juice.

Kids: *They love this minus the trimmings.*

Honey-sweetened breakfast muffins

No sugar, lots of fruit and oatmeal, and they are damned delicious. What more do you want from me?

ALL YOU NEED IS

30g butter

170g runny honey

260g plain or spelt flour

120g oatmeal

2 teaspoons baking powder

1½ teaspoons ground cinnamon

1 apple, grated

2 bananas, mashed

250g blueberries, fresh or frozen

120ml milk

55ml vegetable oil

55ml light olive oil (better still, look out for Good Oil)

3 large eggs

12–16 paper muffin cases

ALL YOU DO IS

1. Pre-heat the oven to 180°C (fan), 200°C, gas mark 6. Line muffin trays with the paper cases.

2. Heat the butter and honey in a pan over a medium heat for a few minutes.

3. Pop into a bowl the flour, oatmeal, baking powder, cinnamon, apple, banana and blueberries. Combine.

4. In another bowl, whisk the milk, oils and eggs and pour into the flour mixture along with the butter and honey. Gently combine. Don't over-mix.

5. Divide the mixture between the muffin cases and bake for 30 minutes. If baking on two shelves, swap the trays halfway through.

These work for breakfast, lunch boxes, picnics, parties, snacks, afternoon tea and so on and so on . . .

Passionate cooked apples

This is something to pop in the fridge at the beginning of the week so that everyone can dip in as they fancy. I use sweet eating apples to avoid adding sugar. Use it to top cereal or yogurt. Or warm it up for pudding with a dollop of ice-cream.

ALL YOU NEED IS

6 sweet eating apples, peeled, cored and sliced
2 ripe passion fruit

ALL YOU DO IS

1. In a covered saucepan gently cook the sliced apples with 3 tablespoons of water.

2. When cooked through and slightly fluffy, after 15 minutes or so, take off the heat and cool.

3. Add the passion fruit and pop in the fridge. Yum!

Babies: *Great for breakfast or puddings, whizzed up.*

All-American blueberry pancakes

Look, you are probably not going to whisk these up every morning before the school run, but for a lazy Sunday morning or special-treat brekkie, they are the business.

ALL YOU NEED IS

150g white spelt or plain flour

1 teaspoon baking powder

60g caster sugar

1 egg

150ml milk

250g blueberries

a big knob of butter

ALL YOU DO IS

1. Sift the flour and baking powder into a bowl. Add the sugar.

2. Whisk together the egg and milk, then pour into the dry ingredients. Mix and finally add the blueberries. Pop in the fridge for half an hour if you have time.

3. Melt the butter in a large (non-stick) frying pan. When it starts to bubble, plop a tablespoon of batter per pancake in the pan.

4. Fry for 2 minutes on each side or until golden.

Serve with lots of fruit, sliced banana and honey or crispy bacon and maple syrup.

Breakfast trifle

Yum! This is so simple and doubles as a gorgeous summertime pudding. A serious step up from boring old fruit salad.

ALL YOU NEED IS

1 big banana

250g punnet raspberries

250g punnet strawberries

1 kiwi fruit

2 large ripe passion fruit

... and any other bits of fruit you want to throw in – grapes, mango, pear and pineapple are good

500g large tub of Greek yogurt

1–2 tablespoons dark brown sugar

ALL YOU DO IS

1. Wash and chop your fruit into a fruit salad. Put in a pretty bowl. Cover with Greek yogurt and sprinkle with sugar. Put in the fridge for an hour or until you need it.

Babies: *Whizz together, minus the sugar.*

Parker's cheese on toast

This is my daughter Parker's favourite breakfast. Mega-moreish!

ALL YOU NEED IS

2 tablespoons grated Cheddar cheese

2 teaspoons good-quality pesto

1 large piece of bread, lightly toasted

ALL YOU DO IS

1. Mix the cheese and pesto and pile on top of the toast. Pop under a hot grill for a minute or so, watching it carefully.

Serve with fresh juice for a great start to the day.

Baked breakfast eggs

We love this great-start breakfast that is a lot easier and healthier than a full English. Plus it works really well as a quick tea.

ALL YOU NEED IS

a little butter
1 piece of thick ham
1 large egg
1 tablespoon grated Gruyère cheese
some crusty bread (or toast)

ALL YOU DO IS

1. Rub a little butter inside a ramekin.

2. Break up a slice of ham into the bottom.

3. Crack the egg on top, then sprinkle the cheese over.

4. Bake at 180°C (fan), 200°C, gas mark 6, for 12–15 minutes.

5. Let it cool slightly and wrap a wet napkin around the outside of the ramekin for the kids, in case it is too hot. Serve straight from the oven for adults.

Serve with crusty bread or toast cut into soldiers.

Good morning granola

Obviously if you have a nut allergy this is like a loaded gun, but for the rest of us it is a great start to the day. Full of the good stuff and minus the rubbish that is thrown into most breakfast cereals. It's expensive but worth it. You can also use it as a topping for yogurt or even ice-cream. Pour some into a clean pickle jar, pop a ribbon round and you have a great little gift. It's a bit twee, I know, but I can't help myself.

ALL YOU NEED IS

400g jumbo oats

3 tablespoons olive oil

200ml apple juice

80g whole unblanched almonds

50g flaked almonds

50g walnuts, chopped up a bit

125g sunflower seeds

3 level tablespoons linseeds
   or pumpkin seeds

3 level tablespoons sesame seeds

3 tablespoons flaked, toasted coconut
   (from health-food shops)

1 teaspoon ground cinnamon

100g sultanas

200g dried blueberries

ALL YOU DO IS

1. Line two baking trays with greaseproof paper and pre-heat the oven to 180°C (fan), 200°C, gas mark 6.

2. Throw all the ingredients, apart from the sultanas and blueberries, into a big bowl and mix thoroughly.

3. Spread the muesli over the two trays and bake for 30 minutes or until golden. It is important to stir it up every 10 minutes.

4. Cool slightly and add the dried fruit. Leave to cool completely before storing in a plastic cereal container or airtight jar. Keeps well for up to 2 weeks.

Serve with milk or sprinkled over yogurt and fresh berries.

Kids: *Be careful with the little ones as the whole nuts are a possible choking hazard. Pick them out if necessary.*

Fruit kebabs

Not so much a recipe as a reminder . . . Stick pretty much anything on a stick and kids will eat it. Try the theory out with vegetables, too. Great for picnics and parties.

ALL YOU NEED IS

fruit! (seasonal, about 100g for each kebab)
your favourite yogurt, to serve

bamboo skewers

ALL YOU DO IS

1. Wash, peel and chop your favourite fruit and thread on to the sticks in alternate colours.

2. Serve with yogurt on the side for dipping.

Babies: *Don't give the sticks to the little ones in case an eye ends up on one!*

RED MEAT

My lot eat masses of red meat. I introduced it to the kids at about eight to nine months and, soon after, we could all chow down on a good old bolognese together. Sonny, in particular, seems to crave it. From his first beef stew he has sat up and begged for more.

The key is to use good-quality, lean meat. Kids don't need the fat and neither do you, for that matter. It can put them off for life. I have such vivid memories of school steak and kidney pie made up of pints of thick, brown, soupy gravy, the odd kidney (I still can't eat vital organs) and lumps of gristle and fat masquerading as meat. Disposing of the offensive lumps became the biggest challenge. In the plant pot, in your pencil case, back into your neighbour's pie. Anything but having to swallow it. Once, having run out of strategic hiding places, I was forced to lob one across the dining hall at my strict convent school. It came to rest smack in the Mother Superior's left eye, which thankfully we always suspected was glass, and there it hung for a good twenty minutes before falling back into the Latin teacher's rice pudding. It's not often you can say, 'Saved by the glass eye . . . '

But good meat doesn't come cheap. So it's better to buy it less often but better quality and make it something you all want to eat. Otherwise, you might find bits hiding in your pot-pourri.

Red meat

Tasty tossed lamb with sweet potato

Quick steak stroganoff

Saucy Sicilian meatballs

Sweet marinated pork fillet

Little lamb burgers with sweet potato wedges

Dressing up your steak and chips

Sausage rolls on the run

Pork escalopes in a rich mushroom sauce

Dan's bung-it-in-the-oven bolognese

Minty chops with pea mash

Leave-in-the-oven lamb shanks

Roast mustard pork with apple

Made-up Tuscan sausage stew

A summer Sunday lunch:
  Cold herb roasted beef
  Crisp green mint summer salad
  Crunchy roast potatoes

Serves: **4 adults**   Prep time: **20 minutes**   Cook time: **30 minutes**

Tasty tossed lamb with sweet potato

Yum! This is really tasty, and apart from being a family favourite it is easily good enough to serve as a lunch or light supper for friends.

ALL YOU NEED IS

500g sweet potatoes, peeled and chopped to bite size

olive oil

100g green beans

500g lamb fillets

fresh pesto (just buy it, don't make it)

handful of baby plum or cherry tomatoes, halved

bag of baby spinach and rocket

balsamic vinegar

3 finely chopped spring onions

75g pine kernels, toasted (roasted or dry-fried – but watch out, they suddenly go brown!)

ALL YOU DO IS

1. Pre-heat the oven to 200°C (fan), 220°C, gas mark 7. Drizzle your sweet potato with a little olive oil and roast for about 30 minutes.

2. Cook the green beans in boiling water for 3 minutes, drain and cool under running cold water.

3. Meanwhile, fry or griddle your lamb fillets to taste (15 minutes or so, turning regularly). Wrap in foil and rest for 10 minutes, then slice diagonally and toss thoroughly in the pesto.

Babies: *Whizz the lamb, potato and beans together, with a little stock or boiled water if necessary.*

Kids: *I serve the tomatoes, beans, sweet potato and lamb all tossed together with a sprinkle of pine nuts on top.*

You: *On a big platter, season and dress your leaves with a little olive oil and balsamic vinegar, then scatter over all the other ingredients and serve.*

Quick steak stroganoff

I once spent a long hard winter in Moscow, working on a low-budget movie. It was minus 30 degrees and the way they kept my body temperature up was to feed me hot stroganoff every half-hour and have two large Russian grandmas embrace me tightly in between shots. I couldn't eat stroganoff for years, but will never tire of a big buxom bear hug.

ALL YOU NEED IS

750g rump steak, fat trimmed off

2 tablespoons olive oil

1 large onion, thinly sliced

knob of butter

2 garlic cloves, crushed or chopped

400g portobello mushrooms, sliced

2 teaspoons chopped fresh tarragon

2 tablespoons tomato purée

2 tablespoons Dijon mustard

200ml soured cream

1 tablespoon flat-leaf parsley

pinch or two of paprika

ALL YOU DO IS

1. Cut the steak into finger-width strips and, in a non-stick pan, fry in batches in half the oil on a high heat for 3–4 minutes until golden brown all over. Set aside, cover with foil and keep warm. Wipe the pan with a piece of kitchen roll in between each batch.

2. In the same pan, with the lid on, fry the onion in the butter for 4 minutes until soft. Add the garlic for 1 minute, then the mushrooms and tarragon for a few minutes until the mushrooms are tender. Add the tomato purée. Stir and add the mustard, then put the meat back in.

3. Stir to coat and remove from the heat. Stir in the soured cream.

Serve with tagliatelle or basmati rice.

Babies: *Chop up nice and small.*

You: *Season on your plate. Scatter some parsley and a pinch of paprika over.*

Saucy Sicilian meatballs

This one was passed down from a friend of the family and it has now become a firm favourite with all of us. My lot love it for its tangy, lemon twist on the normal meatballs in tomato sauce; and me, I love it because I can prepare the whole thing the day before. A good hearty, healthy option too.

ALL YOU NEED IS

For the meatballs:

60g fresh breadcrumbs

500g lean minced beef

2 garlic cloves, crushed

1 tablespoon fresh thyme leaves

zest of 1 unwaxed lemon, finely grated

45g Parmesan cheese, finely grated

¼ teaspoon ground nutmeg

2 medium eggs, beaten

plain or spelt flour for coating

splash of olive oil

For the sauce:

1 large onion

1 celery stick

1 large carrot, all finely chopped

splash of olive oil

2 x 400g tins chopped tomatoes

2 tablespoons tomato purée

250ml low-salt vegetable stock

2 tablespoons red split lentils

ALL YOU DO IS

1. Put the breadcrumbs, mince, garlic, thyme, lemon zest, Parmesan and nutmeg into a bowl. Add the eggs, mix, then, using a spoon and your hands, form into balls (about two bites in size). Roll in flour and put in the fridge until needed.

2. Pre-heat the oven to 180°C (fan), 200°C, gas mark 6. In an ovenproof pan, fry the meatballs in a splash of olive oil, in 2 batches, turning until brown on all sides. (Keep them moving by shaking the pan so they don't stick.) If there is fat left in the pan, drain it off. Add the tomato sauce, put a lid on and pop into the oven for 25 minutes.

For the sauce:

1. Just fry the onion, celery and carrot over a high heat, stirring regularly.

2. After 5 minutes, add the tomatoes, purée, stock and lentils.

3. Let it all gently simmer for about 20 minutes.

Babies: *This works really well for babies. The sauce alone is really handy. Freeze any leftovers.*

Kids: *On pasta it's a winner, but the kids love it on a creamy mash too.*

You: *For the adults, I sometimes add a topping of sour cream and some extra Parmesan. Season on your plate.*

Tip: *To stop the meatballs sticking to your hands when rolling, slightly dampen your hands at regular intervals.*

Sweet marinated pork fillet

Seriously good. When I want to show off, this pork is my number-one choice. My other tactic is a low neckline and a push-up bra.

ALL YOU NEED IS

For the marinade:

3 tablespoons freshly squeezed orange juice

1 tablespoon light soy sauce

2 tablespoons maple syrup

1 tablespoon olive oil

1 teaspoon grated ginger

2 garlic cloves, crushed

½ teaspoon Chinese five-spice

olive oil

800g pork fillets, trimmed

1 teaspoon cornflour

350ml chicken stock

ALL YOU DO IS

1. Mix all the marinade ingredients in a large plastic container, add the pork and turn in the marinade to coat all over. Cover and pop in the fridge overnight.

2. When ready, pre-heat the oven to 180°C (fan), 200°C, gas mark 6.

3. In a non-stick frying pan with a splash of olive oil, brown the pork fillets on all sides over a high heat. Then transfer to a roasting tray and roast for about 20–30 minutes. When they're ready, wrap in foil and rest for 5 minutes or so.

4. Meanwhile, mix the cornflour with 2 teaspoons of water and add to the marinade. Using the same frying pan, pour in the marinade mix and let it boil for about 10 minutes. Add the stock and reduce down. Sieve. Slice the pork fillets diagonally and pour the sauce over.

Serve with a squash and sweet potato mash and some steamed bok choi or sexy spinach (p. 138). Season on your plate.

Babies and kids: *They really like the sweetness but I keep the baby's portion sauce-free.*

Makes: **4 adult portions (about 20 mini burgers)**
For the burgers ···⸱ Prep time: **20 minutes** Cook time: **10 minutes**   ❄ **freezable**
For the wedges ···⸱ Prep time: **10 minutes** Cook time: **30–40 minutes**   **(raw)**

Little lamb burgers with sweet potato wedges

My son becomes slightly doglike when a plate of these is offered up. His little mouth, with man-size teeth, drools and he all but sits up and begs for more. I usually make them beforehand and store in the fridge or freezer until needed. Too tasty to give to your dog . . .

ALL YOU NEED IS

For the wedges:
500g sweet potatoes
2 tablespoons olive oil

For the burgers:
2 garlic cloves, crushed
1 teaspoon ground cumin

1 teaspoon ground coriander
500g lean minced lamb
75g bread
a handful of mint leaves (approx. 15g)
4 spring onions, roughly chopped
60g sesame seeds

ALL YOU DO IS

For the wedges:

1. Pre-heat the oven to 180°C (fan), 200°C, gas mark 6.

2. Cut up the sweet potatoes, skin on, into chip-like wedges, drizzle over half the olive oil, toss to coat and roast on a tray for 30–40 minutes, depending on size.

For the burgers:

1. Meanwhile, in the remaining oil, fry the garlic for 1 minute. Then pop it into a bowl along with the cumin, coriander and minced lamb.

2. Whizz the bread, mint and spring onions in a processor to make breadcrumbs and add to the mince. Get your hands in there and mix it all together. Divide into about 20 balls, then, using your hands, form into little patties.

3. Sprinkle the sesame seeds on a plate and press each burger into them to coat. Refrigerate for 10 minutes or until needed. (Or freeze at this stage and defrost thoroughly before cooking.)

4. In a little olive oil, fry the burgers for 5 minutes each side or until cooked through.

Serve with the nutty pomegranate salad on p. 126. Season on your plate.

Serves: **4 adults**

For the steak ···→   Prep time: **15 minutes**   Cook time: **25 minutes**
For the chips ···→   Prep time: **5 minutes**   Cooking time: **30–45 minutes**

Dressing up your steak and chips

This is a reminder of how much everyone at home, of all ages, loves steak and chips. The dressing just makes the grown-ups feel a bit more, well, grown-up.

ALL YOU NEED IS

For the chips:

2 tablespoons vegetable oil

800g potatoes, peeled and sliced into chip shapes

For the steak:

3 shallots, finely chopped

splash of olive oil

1 garlic clove, crushed

100ml white wine or chicken stock

50ml double cream

1 tablespoon Dijon mustard

1 heaped tablespoon tarragon, roughly chopped

4 good steaks (sirloin, fillet or other)

ALL YOU DO IS

For the chips:

1. Pre-heat the oven to 180°C (fan), 200°C, gas mark 6. Pop the oil on a baking tray and put into the oven to heat.

2. Parboil the potatoes for 5 minutes, then drain well and allow to dry for a minute or so. Toss into the hot oil.

3. Roast for 30–40 minutes until golden, but keep an eye on them. Shake halfway.

For the steak:

1. Fry the shallots in the olive oil until soft, about 10 minutes. Add the garlic and fry gently for a minute, then pour in the wine or stock and simmer for 3–4 minutes. (If you want to pre-prepare, stop and store at this point.)

2. Reduce the heat and add the cream, mustard and tarragon.

3. Meanwhile, griddle, fry or barbecue your steaks on a high heat, as you like them; rest for 5 minutes, then drizzle on your creamy dressing. Season on your plate.

Serve with a green salad for you and some green beans and ketchup for them.

Babies: *Whizz all together or chop up small. (Use the stock, not wine.)*

Sausage rolls on the run

These are brilliant for quick teas, parties, picnics and lunch boxes. Make plenty, as they are always polished off by the grown-ups. I buy the pastry, so the whole thing is a bit of a cheat really . . . So shoot me.

ALL YOU NEED IS
375g pack ready-rolled puff pastry sheet
6 organic sausages
1 egg yolk
1 tablespoon milk
handful of sesame seeds

ALL YOU DO IS
1. Pre-heat the oven to 200°C (fan), 220°C, gas mark 7. Unroll the pastry and cut it down the middle lengthways.

2. Remove the skin from the sausages, then place them, evenly spaced, down each length of pastry and cut the pastry across so that each sausage sits on its own square. Mix the yolk and milk and use as a glue on the edge of each pastry square, like an envelope, then wrap them up (like a sausage roll, obviously). Press the edges gently together and lay joined-side down on a lightly oiled oven tray.

3. Brush the tops with the rest of the egg mix and sprinkle some sesame seeds on top.

4. Bake for 25–30 minutes or until golden. Serve hot, if you can.

Babies and kids: *Great finger food. I serve them with a plateful of chopped raw veggies – and ketchup, of course.*

Pork escalopes in a rich mushroom sauce

If the kids like mushrooms, they will love this. If not – e.g. my daughter Parker – then I just don't pour the sauce over. Simple and delicious for the grown-ups.

ALL YOU NEED IS

2 tablespoons spelt or plain flour

3 teaspoons dried sage

4 x 150g pork escalopes

2 tablespoons olive oil

1 onion, chopped

4 field or portobello mushrooms, sliced

2 tablespoons sherry vinegar

200ml crème fraîche

ALL YOU DO IS

1. Mix the flour and sage and coat the pork. Fry in half the oil until golden, 4–5 minutes each side. Keep warm.

2. In the same pan, heat the rest of the oil and fry the onion. Cook until soft, approximately 10 minutes, then add the mushrooms and cook for a further 5 minutes. Add the sherry vinegar and let it bubble away for a few minutes. Just before serving, add the crème fraîche and heat through.

Pour the sauce over and serve with sexy spinach (p. 138) and tagliatelle. Season on your plate.

Babies: *Whizz or chop up.*

Dan's bung-it-in-the-oven bolognese

Dan's rather grumpy Italian grandfather, 'Pop', would bang on about 'the holy trinity' – fried onion, celery and carrot. It is the basis of all great Italian sauces. Well, he's right, if a little repetitive. This sauce is really rich and the oven does all the work, which is why Dan likes cooking it and Sonny loves eating it . . .

ALL YOU NEED IS

For the holy trinity:

1 celery stick

1 onion

1 carrot, all finely chopped

splash of olive oil

500g lean minced beef

2 x 400g tins chopped tomatoes

200g tube tomato purée

1 bay leaf

1 teaspoon dried oregano

1 tablespoon balsamic vinegar

big pinch of ground nutmeg

4 tablespoons milk

50g Parmesan, grated

ALL YOU DO IS

1. Pre-heat the oven to 160°C (fan), 180°C, gas mark 4.

2. Fry the holy trinity in the oil until softened, in an ovenproof dish that you can transfer to the oven later.

3. Add the mince and stir for 5 minutes until it browns.

4. Add everything else (except the milk and Parmesan) and let it come to the boil.

5. Pop it into the oven with the lid on for 1½ hours.

6. Just before serving, stir in the milk.

7. Spoon over your favourite pasta. Sprinkle with Parmesan. Season on your plate.

Babies: *Make extra for the freezer.*

Minty chops with pea mash

Green mash and meat you can gnaw on like a dog . . . Need I say more?

ALL YOU NEED IS

1 tablespoon lemon juice

1 tablespoon honey

20g fresh mint, chopped
  (save half for the mash)

1 tablespoon olive oil

8 lamb loin chops or cutlets
  (approx. 100g each)

For the mash:

600g potatoes, peeled and cut up

600g frozen peas

1–2 tablespoons olive oil

150g half-fat organic crème fraîche

half the mint from above

ALL YOU DO IS

1. Mix the lemon juice, honey, half the mint and the tablespoon of olive oil in a bowl. Add the chops, turn them over in the mixture and leave in the fridge for up to 3 hours.

2. Boil the potatoes in one pan, peas in another. Cook both until tender. Drain.

3. Mash the potatoes with a drizzle of olive oil. Whizz the peas, crème fraîche and the rest of the mint into a purée using a hand blender or food processor. Then fold the potatoes and pea mix together.

4. When ready, heat a splash of olive oil in a large frying pan or griddle on a high heat. Fry the chops for about 5 minutes each side or until cooked to your liking.

5. Serve the chops on top of the mash. Season on your plate.

Great for all ages.

Babies: *Whizz or chop up to bite size. Make extra mash to freeze.*

Leave-in-the-oven lamb shanks

This is a rich, warm stew that bubbles away in the oven for 3 hours. Which leaves you time to clean the house and your hair.

ALL YOU NEED IS

splash of olive oil

4 lamb shanks (as lean as possible)

For the sauce:

2 large onions, chopped

1 stick of celery, chopped

450g organic carrots, cut into large chunks

4 garlic cloves, crushed

handful of fresh rosemary leaves

400ml low-salt vegetable stock

2 x 400g tins chopped tomatoes

2 star anise

freshly ground black pepper

2 tablespoons runny honey

ALL YOU DO IS

1. Pre-heat the oven to 160°C (fan), 180°C, gas mark 4.

2. Using a large casserole dish, heat a splash of olive oil and brown the lamb shanks, in batches, all over. Then remove.

3. Throw your onions and celery into the dish to fry a little before adding the garlic, carrots and rosemary. Fry on a medium heat for 5 minutes or so.

4. Now add the stock, tomatoes, star anise and a grind or two of pepper. Bring to the boil. Return the meat to the dish. Put the shanks in with the bones sticking out of the liquid and trickle the honey over the exposed meat and bone.

5. Stick a lid on, pop it in the oven and cook for 3 hours.

Serve with your favourite mash and a big bowl of minted peas. Season on your plate.

Babies and kids: *This is a favourite with babies and kids alike. I just take it off the bone for them and shred the babies' portions. It freezes really well.*

Tip: *You could make this up to 2 days in advance and store in the fridge.*

Roast mustard pork with apple

This is a great alternative to roast chicken, but it is so much quicker to cook. I serve it with simple roast parsnips, which should only take 30 minutes in the hot oven you need for the pork.

ALL YOU NEED IS

knob of butter (approx. 30g)

1 teaspoon brown sugar

4 apples, peeled and thinly sliced

2 medium onions, thickly sliced

olive oil

freshly ground black pepper

800g pork fillet, trimmed

5 teaspoons Dijon mustard

100ml low-salt vegetable stock

125ml apple juice

ALL YOU DO IS

1. Pre-heat the oven to 200°C (fan), 220°C, gas mark 7.

2. Melt the butter and brown sugar in a pan. Cook the apples gently for about 10 minutes, turning occasionally. (You can pre-make and reheat.)

3. Put the slices of onion on a roasting tray as a bed for the pork. Drizzle over a little olive oil and grind over some pepper.

4. Smear the pork fillets all over with the mustard and lay on the onion bed. Roast for 20–30 minutes, depending on how you like your pork. Remove the meat, cover with foil and rest for 5 minutes.

5. For the sauce, place the roasting tray on the hob. Roughly chop the cooked onion, add the stock and apple juice. Bring to the boil and bubble away for a few minutes.

6. Thickly slice the pork diagonally and serve with the warm, sweet apples on the side and the sauce over the top. Season on your plate.

Babies: *You can cook the apples without sugar, no problem. Then whizz all together with mash. They love it.*

Made-up Tuscan sausage stew

This casserole is divine. Given to me by Lucy, a brilliant make-up artist and clearly an even better cook. Her twist of adding pesto brings out all those Italian flavours and my family can't get enough of it. Sonny, in particular, is like a wild animal for this one.

ALL YOU NEED IS

6 of your fave sausages (450g or so)

1 tablespoon olive oil

1 medium onion, chopped

1 large carrot, chopped

1 stick celery, chopped

1 medium red pepper, chopped

1 organic chicken stock cube

2 x 400g tins chopped tomatoes

1 x 400g tin cannellini beans, drained and rinsed

1 tablespoon tomato purée

1 bay leaf

1 teaspoon dried oregano

1 tablespoon good-quality pesto (fresh is best)

ALL YOU DO IS

1. Pre-heat the oven to 180°C (fan), 200°C, gas mark 6. Brown the sausages in a casserole dish in the oil for 5 minutes , then cut each sausage in 4. When they are well on their way, add the chopped onion, carrot, celery and pepper to soften. Add a little more olive oil if you need to, and cook for 10 more minutes.

2. Dissolve the stock cube in just a mug of boiling water and add to the pot along with the tinned tomatoes, cannellini beans, tomato purée, bay leaf and oregano. Bring to simmering point and cover.

3. Cook in the oven with the lid on for 30–40 minutes. When ready, stir in the pesto.

Serve on mash in winter and pasta (tagliatelle) in summer. Season on your plate.

Babies: *Whizz or chop up.*

A summer Sunday lunch
Cold herb roasted beef

This is so easy to prepare, but delights everyone around the table. It's a simple summer twist on a traditional Sunday roast. The freshness of the herb crust with the crunchy roast potatoes, minty veg and the creamy mayonnaise is a winner. Not cheap, but it is sublime.

ALL YOU NEED IS

1.2–1.5kg beef fillet, trimmed

120ml olive oil

2 tablespoons fresh thyme leaves

3 garlic cloves, finely chopped

80ml balsamic vinegar

freshly ground black pepper

1 large bunch flat-leaf parsley, finely chopped

2 or 3 handfuls of mixed herbs (tarragon, thyme, oregano), finely chopped

garlic mayonnaise (from all good supermarkets)

ALL YOU DO IS

1. Marinate the beef fillet for as long as possible in the oil, thyme, garlic and balsamic vinegar. Give it a twist of black pepper. Cover well and place in the fridge. Turn the meat when you remember. Take out of the fridge an hour before cooking if possible.

2. Pre-heat the oven to 220°C (fan), 240°C, gas mark 9. Drain the beef and pat dry with a little kitchen paper. Put it on to a roasting tray and then into the middle of a very hot oven for 15 minutes. Turn over and cook for another 15 minutes for medium. Kids like it well cooked, so allow some extra time. Remove from the oven and let it rest and cool (about 40 minutes).

3. For the crust, place half the chopped herbs on a large piece of cling film. Put the beef on top, pressing down to coat. Scatter the remaining herbs on top. Then wrap tightly in cling film and refrigerate for an hour.

4. When you are ready, remove the cling film, slice thickly and serve at room temperature, with spoonfuls of garlic mayonnaise.

Serve with crunchy roast potatoes and a crisp green mint summer salad (p. 68).

For the salad ⋯⟩ Serves: **6 adults** Prep time: **10 minutes** Cook time: **5 minutes**
For the roast potatoes ⋯⟩ Serves: **6 adults** Prep time: **10 minutes** Cook time: **50 minutes**

Crisp green mint summer salad

ALL YOU NEED IS

200g French beans
350g frozen peas
250g bunch asparagus
225g bag young leaf spinach, washed
handful of fresh mint, chopped
    (approx. 15g)

For the dressing:

3 tablespoons olive oil
1 tablespoon white wine vinegar
squeeze of lemon
1 teaspoon Dijon mustard

ALL YOU DO IS

1. Add the French beans and peas to a pan of boiling water and cook for 5 minutes, adding the asparagus halfway through. Drain and refresh under running cold water.

2. Throw the veg in a bowl full of your spinach.

3. Whisk together all the dressing ingredients and pour over the salad just before serving. Scatter the fresh mint over.

Kids: *I tend to take the kids' greens out before dressing and seasoning them.*

Crunchy roast potatoes

ALL YOU NEED IS

about 250g of spuds per person

1. No secret here, except that parboiling the potatoes for about 10 minutes and then bashing them about once drained really is worth doing.

2. If you heat your vegetable oil in the oven, that helps too. Season them on your plate.

WHITE MEAT

Fish and chicken are an obvious and sensible choice for family cooking. But the problem comes when you end up putting the same old thing on the plate day after day because it's easy and you don't have to think about it.

But life is short, my friends, and every meal is an opportunity to enjoy yourself. Why have boring pre-prepared fish with little or no flavour when with so little effort you can knock up a salmon frittata or chicken casserole?

The trick is to try a simple but new recipe once a week to start with, slowly building up your repertoire. That way, you will find the ones you like and add them to the usual list you rely on. Keep going until, hopefully, one day you notice that those old faithfuls have been put on the back burner and your family are looking at you eagerly at lunch time, rather than barely noticing the food they eat.

Excited, not bored, is the aim for them and for you. Trust me, it's achievable.

PS Sustainable fish and free-range chicken. Take it seriously. Good for you, good for them. Right?

White meat
(and fish, obviously)

No crust salmon pizza

Salade niçoise

Quick creamy haddock

Orange and ginger chicken casserole

Smoked salmon frittata with horseradish cream

Roast poussin stuffed with raspberry and thyme

Pancetta-wrapped monkfish with creamy roast courgettes

My favourite chicken in mint yogurt

One-pot lemon chicken with thyme rice

Tandoori takeaway

Chinese takeaway:
  Sticky ginger chicken
  Chinese roast broccoli

Simple fish dressing

Cobbled salad

Creamy chicken and ham pie

Chicken souvlaki with peach salsa

Parmesan plaice fingers with soft eggs and asparagus salad

Bob's bay bird

Chicken soup

Serves: **6 adults**   Prep time: **5 minutes (plus 20 minutes for tomato sauce)**
Cook time: **20 minutes**

No crust salmon pizza

Question: How do I get my kids to eat more fish?
Answer: Tell them they're having pizza tonight!

ALL YOU NEED IS

350–400g Italian tomato sauce
   (see Mega-quick Italian
   tomato sauce, p. 175)
3 portobello mushrooms (approx. 200g)
1 tablespoon olive oil
6 salmon fillets, boned

1 tablespoon chives, chopped
handful of chopped basil (approx. 25g)
1 large ball of buffalo mozzarella
handful of pitted olives (approx. 50g):
   the colour is your choice

ALL YOU DO IS

1. Make your tomato sauce. (Or you can cheat and use a good jar.) Then roughly slice the mushrooms and fry in the olive oil until soft.

2. Pre-heat the oven to 200°C (fan), 220°C, gas mark 7. Slice the salmon fillets horizontally and lay out on a pizza stone or a large roasting tray lined with baking paper. Overlap the halved fillets to create a circle for your salmon pizza base.

3. Scatter the mushrooms over the base and cover with the tomato sauce. Sprinkle with the chopped herbs. Then roughly break up the mozzarella and scatter it all over. Throw on a few olives and bake for 20 minutes.

4. Use the paper to slide the pizza on to a big wooden board.

Serve immediately with a green salad and garlic bread (p. 145).

Babies: *Whizz or just break up with a fork (no olives for little mouths).*

Salade niçoise

Don't be scared of salads. This classic works for all the family. A great summer lunch for everyone.

ALL YOU NEED IS

350g new potatoes, skin on, washed

1 large soft lettuce, washed

100g green beans, topped and tailed

12 or so cherry tomatoes, halved

handful of pitted olives

3 tablespoons olive oil

1 tablespoon lemon juice

freshly ground black pepper

4 fresh tuna steaks, 125g each

4 large organic eggs, softly boiled

200g humous

ALL YOU DO IS

1. Boil the potatoes till they fall off the fork, then drain and halve them.

2. Wash the lettuce leaves, rinse and put into a lovely big bowl. Put the potatoes on top.

3. Throw the beans briefly into boiling water. Drain. Add to the bowl.

4. Now add the tomato halves and olives and dress the lot with the olive oil, lemon juice and a grind of pepper.

5. Brush the tuna steaks with a little oil and fry or griddle on a high heat to your taste. (They always need less time than you think, 1 minute or so on each side.) Roughly break up the steaks and scatter on top of the salad.

6. Shell and halve the eggs and place on top.

7. And finally, spoon on dollops of the humous and serve with hot garlic bread (p. 145). Season on your plate.

Babies and kids: *I tend to make the kids' plates up first, before dressing the salad. Hard-boil the eggs for the babies and cook their tuna right through. If whizzing the tuna, beans and potatoes, use a squeeze or two of lemon juice as well.*

Tip: *For a cheaper alternative, use a really good-quality tin or jar of tuna.*

Quick creamy haddock

This is creamy, comforting and very quick to make. I use smoked haddock, but if your lot don't go for that smoky flavour then try it with normal haddock. I can never find the time to make fish pie, but if you serve this with a good mash and some garden peas you won't have to. If one day you do find that extra hour, get a massage.

ALL YOU NEED IS

4 large tomatoes

600g undyed smoked haddock fillet, skinned and boned

handful of fresh basil (about 25g)

freshly ground black pepper

100ml single cream

100g half-fat crème fraîche

50g Parmesan, grated

50g Gruyère cheese, grated

ALL YOU DO IS

1. Pre-heat the oven to 180°C (fan), 200°C, gas mark 6.

2. Skin the tomatoes in a bowl by pouring boiling water over them. Leave for a minute or so, then rub off the skin with a cloth. Halve and deseed them and roughly chop.

3. Cut the haddock up into bite-size pieces and spread out in a ceramic ovenproof dish. Scatter on the tomatoes and tear the basil over.

4. Grind in a little pepper and pour the cream and crème fraîche over. Finally, scatter the 2 cheeses on top.

5. Bake for 30–35 minutes.

As suggested above, serve with chive mash (p. 137) and garden peas. Even quicker and just as delicious, serve with crusty bread and a watercress salad.

Babies: *Great whizzed with mash and peas. (Start them on unsmoked fish.)*

Orange and ginger chicken casserole

This is warming and stupidly popular in my house. I often cook it when I have loads of stuff to do. With a bit of preparation, I can rush around while this bubbles away in the oven, filling the house with its delicious smells. Serve it to the kids, then pop a lid on. It keeps warm for ages, until you have a quiet house and a glass of wine to hand.

ALL YOU NEED IS

For the marinade:

1 teaspoon ground cumin

1 teaspoon finely grated fresh ginger

2 garlic cloves, crushed

zest of 1 orange

3 tablespoons olive oil

6 (organic) chicken thighs, skin off

1 large onion, chopped

3 large carrots, roughly chopped

150ml (organic) chicken stock

juice of 2 oranges

½ tablespoon olive oil

ALL YOU DO IS

1. Mix all of the marinade ingredients in a bowl and toss the chicken into it. Cover and leave in the fridge for at least 30 minutes – longer is good.

2. Pre-heat the oven to 180°C (fan), 200°C, gas mark 6, then transfer the chicken and marinade into a hot, non-stick frying pan and seal on both sides, which will only take a few minutes.

3. Meanwhile, in the oil, fry the onion and carrot in a separate, ovenproof casserole dish on the hob, until soft, about 10 minutes.

4. Combine everything by putting the browned chicken, stock and orange juice into the casserole dish with the onions and carrots. Give it all a good stir, cover and cook for 45–60 minutes: when the chicken is pierced, the juice should run clear.

Babies: *Take the meat off the bone before whizzing for the baby. Freezes brilliantly.*

You and the kids: *Serve to all ages with a pile of sweet potatoes roasted in their jackets, or a pile of yummy greens.*

Smoked salmon frittata with horseradish cream

Great for lunch, picnics or an easy tea. You can serve the kids' portions warm and have yours at room temperature later with a green salad and the dip. All the food groups in one slice. Nice.

ALL YOU NEED IS

500g new potatoes, skin on, washed
300g smoked salmon
8 large eggs
2 tablespoons fresh dill, chopped
150g frozen petits pois
freshly ground black pepper
splash of olive oil

For the dip:

3 tablespoons half-fat crème fraîche
3 teaspoons creamed horseradish

ALL YOU DO IS

1. Pre-heat the oven to 180°C (fan), 200°C, gas mark 6.

2. Boil the potatoes until tender. Drain, then slice thickly. Cut the salmon into strips.

3. Beat the eggs a little and add the salmon, potatoes, dill, frozen petits pois and a grind of pepper.

4. Heat a splash of oil in a large non-stick frying pan. Pour in the egg mix and cook on the hob for about 15–20 minutes, then pop it into the oven for a further 5–10 minutes, until set. Watch out for the hot handle. Slice and serve.

5. For the dip, just mix the crème fraîche and horseradish and season.

Babies and kids: *Great finger food.*

Roast poussin stuffed with raspberry and thyme

These are a fantastic alternative to roast chicken. There is something deeply satisfying about eating a whole 'thing'. The raspberries add a real sense of occasion to this dish. Very quick to prepare.

ALL YOU NEED IS

75g butter

8 sprigs thyme (at least)

120g raspberries

4 poussins (450g each)

8 slices smoked pancetta

50ml or ½ glass dry sherry (optional)

100ml chicken stock

3 tablespoons redcurrant jelly

ALL YOU DO IS

1. Pre-heat the oven to 200°C (fan), 220°C, gas mark 7.

2. Pop a knob of butter, 2–3 sprigs of thyme and a few raspberries inside each bird.

3. Lay a couple of slices of the pancetta over the breasts and put on a roasting tray.

4. Roast for 50 minutes, then cover with foil and rest on a plate for 10 minutes, first pouring any juices from the birds into the tray.

5. For the sauce, just heat your tray on the hob, adding the sherry, stock and jelly.

6. Scrape all the good stuff up and bubble away on a high temperature for 5 minutes or until the alcohol has burned off (if using it) and the jelly melted.

Serve all the birds on one big plate and the sauce on the side. Lovely with my roast parsnips (p. 130) in winter or salads in summer.

Babies: *Obviously take the meat off the bone and whizz with some veg and mash (no sherry, please!)*

Pancetta-wrapped monkfish with creamy roast courgettes

Parker thinks monkfish is a silly name for a fish (a fair comment), but it's a treat and seems to appeal to all ages. You can use any other firm white fish with a more sensible name if you prefer.

ALL YOU NEED IS

4 courgettes, thinly sliced

1 tablespoon olive oil

4 monkfish fillets (130g each)

freshly ground black pepper

juice of a big lemon

8 rashers of pancetta

4 tablespoons crème fraîche

ALL YOU DO IS

1. Pre-heat the oven to 200°C (fan), 220°C, gas mark 7. Scatter the courgette slices over a baking tray and drizzle with olive oil.

2. Season the fish with some pepper and a quick squeeze of lemon juice.

3. Wrap each fillet (except the baby's portion) in 2 slices of pancetta and place on top of the courgettes.

4. Bake for 15 minutes, then add the rest of the lemon juice and dot the crème fraîche over the courgettes, stirring gently. Cook for a further 10 minutes.

5. Serve on top of the creamy courgettes.

How about green beans on the side? Season on your plate.

Babies: *Don't wrap the baby's portion in pancetta. Whizz with the courgettes.*

My favourite chicken in mint yogurt

This makes a great summer salad for us and all kids love it. I tend to serve the children when the chicken is warm and let ours cool. You can even make it beforehand and store it in the fridge, as it is at its best when cold. Brilliant for picnics, too.

ALL YOU NEED IS

350g Greek yogurt

2 handfuls of fresh mint, chopped

4 (organic) chicken breast fillets

ALL YOU DO IS

1. Mix the yogurt and mint together and spoon it over the chicken, tucking as much of the herby yogurt in the nooks and crannies of the meat as possible.

2. Bake on a shallow baking tray at 200°C (fan), 220°C, gas mark 7 for about 30–40 minutes or until the topping is brown and the chicken cooked through.

3. Leave to cool slightly, then slice diagonally. Season on your plate.

Babies: *Lovely whizzed up with mash.*

Kids: *Serve to the kids on rice or with green beans in pitta bread.*

One-pot lemon chicken with thyme rice

This is a warming, tangy dish that can bubble away in the oven and then be put straight on the table. So I use my favourite casserole dish. Serve with a green salad and some crusty bread if friends are over, but it's great as it is. A family classic!

ALL YOU NEED IS

6 (organic) chicken pieces (thighs and breasts work well)

1 tablespoon olive oil

1 large onion, chopped

150g pack Italian pancetta cubes

2 large garlic cloves

280g brown basmati rice

700ml (organic) chicken stock

juice and zest of 1½ lemons (unwaxed)

2–3 bushy sprigs thyme

250g frozen broad beans (a couple of handfuls)

freshly ground black pepper

4 litre ovenproof casserole dish, with lid

ALL YOU DO IS

1. Set the oven at 200°C (fan), 220°C, gas mark 7. In your casserole dish, brown the chicken pieces in a little olive oil. Remove and set aside.

2. In the same oil, fry the onion and pancetta for a couple of minutes. Then crush the garlic and add. Keep stirring for a minute, being careful not to burn the garlic.

3. Put the rice in and stir to coat.

4. Add the stock, lemon juice and zest, thyme, the broad beans and a twist of black pepper.

5. Bring to the boil, then pop the chicken pieces on top. Put a lid on and stick in the oven for 50 minutes.

6. Serve straight from your dish. Season on your plate.

Babies and kids: *This is definitely on my kids' top-three favourites list. (Be careful of hot pot on little hands.)*

Tandoori takeaway

This is mega-quick and, let's face it, a bit of a cheat, but hey, who's watching? It's very tasty and takes about the same time to prepare as a phone call to your local takeaway.

ALL YOU NEED IS

1 medium onion, finely chopped

2 tablespoons tandoori paste

250g Greek yogurt

6 (organic) chicken thighs, skin taken off

ALL YOU DO IS

1. In a large bowl, mix the onion, paste and yogurt.

2. Add the chicken and mix to coat. Pop into the fridge overnight if possible, or for at least 3 hours.

3. Transfer to an ovenproof dish and cook at 200°C (fan), 220°C, gas mark 7 for 40 minutes.

Serve with rice, peas and fresh chopped mint, mixed together. Or makes great picnic finger food.

Babies: *I do everything the same, but when it comes to adding the tandoori paste use just enough to colour the yogurt slightly. Mind you, Sonny loves it prepared as above.*

Chinese takeaway

I hate all the junk that goes into most Chinese fast-food options. So, for a healthier, frankly tastier option, try this quick Chinese fix.

Sticky ginger chicken

ALL YOU NEED IS

3 globes stem ginger (from a jar)

2 tablespoons runny honey

2 tablespoons light soy sauce

2 garlic cloves, crushed

2 limes

6 (organic) chicken thighs, skinned

ALL YOU DO IS

1. Drain and finely chop the ginger. Pop into a shallow ovenproof ceramic dish with the honey, soy sauce, garlic, the zest of 2 limes and juice of 1 lime.

2. Put the chicken in and toss well. Refrigerate overnight if possible (not essential).

3. When ready, pre-heat the oven to 210°C (fan), 230°C, gas mark 8. Spread out the thighs in one layer and cook for 30–40 minutes, until the juices run clear.

Serve with basmati rice and season on your plate.

Chinese roast broccoli

ALL YOU NEED IS

300g head of broccoli

1 teaspoon coriander seeds

2 tablespoons olive oil

ALL YOU DO IS

1. Cut the broccoli into florets and lay out on a roasting tray.

2. Crush the coriander seeds and sprinkle over the florets. Pour plenty of olive oil over them and bake for 20 minutes at 210°C (fan), 230°C, gas mark 8. They will burn a little, but don't worry, that's the best bit. Serve immediately.

Babies: *Just chop up and serve with steamed broccoli instead.*

Simple fish dressing

The dash of soy in this delicious, simple dressing comes from Giorgio, my father-in-law, a rugged Italian old stallion who lives on a hill in Tuscany. He cooks us fish in his outside oven and serves the dressing over it. It tastes like summer itself.

ALL YOU NEED IS

25g (big handful) chopped fresh parsley

10g (small handful) chopped fresh mint

200ml olive oil

juice of 3 large lemons

1 dessertspoon light soy sauce

175g per portion of any fish fillets (tuna, cod, sea bass, etc.)

a sprinkle of dried chilli (optional)

ALL YOU DO IS

1. Combine the herbs, oil, lemon juice and soy. Marinate the fish fillets in half this dressing, in the fridge, for an hour if you have time. Save the rest of the dressing.

2. Remove the fillets from the marinade and either whack them on the barbecue or fry for 3–4 minutes each side, over a medium heat.

3. To serve, pour over the other half of the dressing. Season on your plate.

This is great with a simple salad and some boiled potatoes broken up and dressed with lemon and olive oil.

Babies: *Just whizz together the marinated cooked fish and potatoes, but don't add the final dressing.*

You: *Crumble a pinch of dried chilli over your portion.*

Cobbled salad

Fill a huge, flat plate with a bit of everything – feel free to use up anything going begging in the fridge – and serve with crusty bread and tahini dressing on the side. Healthy as hell and the kids love that picnic feel.

ALL YOU NEED IS

1 small cos lettuce, leaves washed

1 big handful of baby spinach
  or watercress

2 avocados, sliced

½ cucumber, cubed

2 carrots, grated

10 cherry tomatoes, halved

2 eggs, hard-boiled, quartered

100g frozen sweetcorn, cooked

2 tablespoons pitted olives
  (black or green)

100g Emmenthal cheese, sliced

8 rashers of pancetta

2 skinless (organic) chicken breasts,
  roughly chopped, about 250g in total

For the dressing:

1 tablespoon tahini

juice of ½ lemon

1 dessertspoon white wine vinegar

1 teaspoon grain mustard

2 tablespoons olive oil

1 tablespoon water

ALL YOU DO IS

1. On a big plate lay out the lettuce leaves, spinach, avocados, cucumber, carrot, tomatoes, egg, sweetcorn, olives and cheese.

2. Fry the pancetta on a high heat for 5 minutes, until golden and crisp, cool slightly, then add to the salad plate. In the same pan, stir-fry the chicken till cooked through (7 minutes-ish) and add to the salad.

3. Whisk all the dressing ingredients and serve on the side.

Babies: *Put together their favourite combo. Sonny's is chicken, avocado, egg and corn. Chop or whizz with a tiny bit of dressing or olive oil.*

Creamy chicken and ham pie

There's something about a good pie. Everything is in there, I guess. This one is extremely tasty and pretty easy to achieve. Make two if friends are over and they will forever call you a domestic goddess.

ALL YOU NEED IS

1 tablespoon olive oil

1 leek, finely chopped

2–3 (organic) chicken breasts (approx. 350g), chopped to bite size

1 (organic) chicken stock cube

375g pack fresh ready-rolled shortcrust pastry

a little flour for rolling out

4 slices of serrano ham (or prosciutto), cut into strips

4 or 5 basil leaves

freshly ground black pepper

6 tablespoons double cream

1 egg, lightly beaten

ALL YOU DO IS

1. Pre-heat the oven to 200°C (fan), 220°C, gas mark 7.

2. In the oil, sweat the leeks for 5 minutes, then brown the chicken for 5 more minutes. Set aside. Mix the stock cube with a mug of boiling water. Set aside.

3. Unroll the pastry and cut out the biggest circle you can (around 22cm – the size of a dinner plate – should work). Use it to line a smaller, greased loose-bottomed cake tin – around 18cm ideally. The pastry should form a vessel for the filling, but don't stress: it is meant to be 'rustic'. Use a little flour and reshape and roll out the leftover pastry to make a lid for the pie, so that it 'sort-of' fits.

4. Arrange the leeks, chicken and ham inside the pastry case. Tear up and scatter the basil and give a grind of pepper. Then spoon over the cream and 4 tablespoons of stock. Pop on your pastry lid and brush it all over with a little egg.

5. Place the tin on a baking tray (it often leaks a bit, but fear not) and put into the oven, on the top shelf, for 20 minutes. Then reduce the heat to 180°C (fan), 200°C, gas mark 6 for a further 20 minutes, until the pastry is golden. Leave it to settle for 5 minutes before unmoulding from the tin and cutting.

Babies: *Great once they can use a fork or spoon.*

Chicken souvlaki with peach salsa

It's on a stick, so the kids will automatically love it. I hope you get to do this on the barbecue, but even if you don't, the fresh fruity salsa makes it feel like summer is here anyway. A great summer party recipe in minutes.

ALL YOU NEED IS

600g (organic) chicken breasts, skin off

1 tablespoon olive oil

½ teaspoon sweet smoked paprika

1 tablespoon fresh thyme leaves

freshly ground black pepper

4 peaches, stoned and peeled

2 tablespoons lime juice

½ small red onion, finely chopped

6 bamboo skewers

ALL YOU DO IS

1. Pre-heat the oven to 200°C , 220°C, gas mark 7, or fire up the barbecue.

2. Chop the chicken into big bite-size pieces and put into a bowl with the oil, paprika, thyme and a grind of pepper. Pop into the fridge until you need it (an hour at least, if possible). Soak some wooden skewers in water for a few minutes.

3. Chop the peaches and dress with the lime juice and onion.

4. Thread the chicken on to the skewers (about 5 chunks each) and pop on the barbecue or into the oven till cooked through, about 20 minutes.

Serve with the peach salsa and season on your plate.

Parmesan plaice fingers with soft eggs and asparagus salad

This is light and delicate. Unlike me . . .

ALL YOU NEED IS

5 tablespoons olive oil

1 tablespoon lemon juice

1 teaspoon light soy sauce

1 heaped tablespoon chopped mint

1 heaped tablespoon chopped parsley

2 whole eggs, plus 2 egg yolks

freshly ground black pepper

2 handfuls of breadcrumbs
  (whizz up something from the bread bin)

2 tablespoons Parmesan, grated

4 tablespoons spelt or plain four

2 whole plaice (or sole) (280g)

250g fresh asparagus

2 big handfuls baby leaf spinach leaves

ALL YOU DO IS

1. For the dressing, just shake together 3 tablespoons of olive oil with the lemon juice, soy sauce and herbs.

2. Soft-boil the 2 whole eggs, plunge into cold water and shell.

3. Beat the egg yolks with 1 tablespoon of olive oil, a tablespoon of water and a grind of pepper.

4. In a separate bowl, mix the breadcrumbs and Parmesan together. Put the flour in another bowl.

5. Cut the fish into finger-width strips (I use scissors) and dip, to coat, first into the flour, then the yolk mix and finally the breadcrumbs. Fry in another tablespoon of oil for 1–2 minutes on each side until golden. Drain on kitchen paper.

6. Steam the asparagus until tender but still slightly crisp.

7. When ready to serve, you can pop the shelled eggs into a bowl of warm water to warm through.

Babies and kids: *Great finger food. Just lay off the spinach and dressing for the kids.*

Bob's bay bird

My friend Bob always chucks a chook in the oven when we stay with him. He has a huge bay bush in his wonderful country garden and gathers handfuls of it to stuff the bird. The whole house fills with the smell. It's the best roast chicken I know.

ALL YOU NEED IS

1 large onion, peeled and thickly sliced

1 garlic bulb

1 (organic) chicken

10 fresh bay leaves (torn) or 5 dried ones

splash of olive oil

freshly ground black pepper

splash of balsamic vinegar

glass of white wine (for the gravy)

ALL YOU DO IS

1. Pre-heat the oven to 180°C (fan), 200°C, gas mark 6.

2. Lay the thick slices of onion on a roasting tray as a bed for the bird to sit on. Roughly break up the garlic bulb into cloves and add.

3. Remove any giblets from the bird so that you can stuff all the bay leaves into the carcass. Then pop it on to the onion and garlic bed. Once in place, put 2 tablespoons of water inside the bird.

4. Drizzle some olive oil over the whole thing. Grind a little pepper over and bung in the oven for 1 hour, 15 minutes or so, depending on the weight of the bird (45 minutes per kg, plus 20 minutes).

5. When it's cooked and the juices run clear, leave the bird to rest while you make the quick and delicious gravy. Put the roasting tray and juices on the hob.

6. Roughly chop the cooked onion in the pan and squeeze out the garlic, throwing the husks away. Add a splash of balsamic vinegar and pour in the wine, boiling it all over a high heat for a few minutes until the alcohol has evaporated. Serve the gravy separately. Season on your plate.

Babies: *A classic to whizz with a bit of everything.*

Chicken soup

Everyone needs chicken soup in their lives. It's restorative, comforting and mega-tasty. Where I live in north London, GPs prescribe it for almost all ailments. Colds, tummy bugs, broken bones . . . Perhaps it should be available on the NHS?

ALL YOU NEED IS

2 (organic) chicken legs, skin off
180g sweet potato, chopped
2 large carrots, chopped
2 celery sticks, chopped
1 medium onion, chopped

1 bay leaf
zest of 1 lemon
1 litre low-salt vegetable stock
1 tablespoon fresh parsley, chopped

ALL YOU DO IS

1. Put all the ingredients except the parsley into a large saucepan, bring to the boil and simmer for an hour with the lid on.

2. Take out the chicken legs and allow to cool enough to handle them. Then shred the chicken, discarding the bones, and put back into the soup.

Babies: *Whizz for the tiny ones, to remove the bits.*

You: *Serve with the parsley scattered on top. Season your own bowl.*

NO MEAT

My family are split into two very different camps. One half are vegetarians; the other half kill, skin and gut their lunch themselves.

The ones that love to stroke animals . . .

When I was about five we had a crowd of family and friends over for Sunday lunch, and suddenly we heard screeching worthy of a Greek tragedy. Everyone rushed to discover my Auntie Twinkle trying to give the kiss of life to a bluebottle that she had fished out of the loo. I watched this grown woman weep as she gently massaged the fly's tummy (do flies have tummies?) and, bugger me, it buzzed back to life and flew off to live another day and find another toilet.

The ones that love to eat them . . .

My dad used to live on a remote farm surrounded by woodland, with gentle deer that ventured close to the house. Again it was a Sunday family lunch, and among us was a young cousin from overseas who had taken a shine to the friendly deer that greeted her every morning. She named her favourites Bella and Bob. As we all tucked into our delicious roast lamb (or was it?), my dad announced the reason Bella had stopped appearing. 'Because you've just eaten her, of course.' At which point our cousin threw up on the Brussels sprouts, and Auntie Dawn (Auntie Twinkle's sister) tried to ring the police to report the 'murder'. We calmed her down with a dry sherry, and as we had eaten the evidence we all agreed it would be hard to prosecute. So we went ahead with pudding on the understanding Dad didn't shoot anything with a name again.

As for me, I love vegetarian food . . . as long as I can have pancetta on top.

No meat

A great veggie tart

Simple stuffed roast peppers

The idiot-proof roast butternut squash soup

Potato dauphinois

Baby carrots with lemon thyme

Runner beans in tomato sauce

Nutty pomegranate salad

Red rice salad

Roast Parmesan parsnips

Molto buono beans

Warm winter soup

Mish-mash

Sexy garlic spinach

Sweet carrot and lentil soup

Roast garlic and lemon new potatoes

Garlic bread

Onion marmalade

A great veggie tart

My baby sister, Elisa, has been a vegetarian since she was a little girl. (Despite her evil big sister trying to slip bacon into every lunch box.) I'm not sure why I struggled so much with the idea of life without meat, but I have finally managed to accept she is her own person. She will never eat a burger, has legs twice as long as mine and believes she can change the world through the medium of paper recycling.

ALL YOU NEED IS

300g shortcrust pastry,
    ready-rolled or your own: you choose

175g leeks, finely sliced and rinsed

knob of butter (20g)

2 handfuls of frozen petits pois (100g)

200g baby leaf spinach,
    washed and roughly chopped

2 large eggs

200g half-fat crème fraîche

100ml milk

90g Gruyère cheese, grated

freshly ground black pepper

a 24cm x 3cm-ish tart tin

ALL YOU DO IS

1. Pre-heat the oven to 200°C (fan), 220°C, gas mark 7.

2. Roll out the pastry and line the tart tin. Prick the base with a fork. Bake blind (with baking beans or rice on top of greaseproof paper) for 15 minutes, then remove the paper and beans and bake for a further 5 minutes. Set aside.

3. For the filling, simply fry the leeks in a knob of butter until soft. Stir in the frozen petits pois for a minute, then add the spinach for a couple of minutes with a lid on. Sieve off any liquid and pop into the pastry case.

4. Gently whisk together the eggs, crème fraîche, milk, cheese and a grind of pepper. Spoon over the veggie filling.

5. Reduce the oven temperature to 180°C (fan), 200°C, gas mark 6 and bake, on a baking tray, for 25–30 minutes or until the top is golden and set.

Serve hot or cold.

Babies: *I just break up Sonny's and give him a spoon.*

Tip: *To make life easier, bake the case in advance. It will keep in the fridge overnight. Or make the whole tart the day before and warm through.*

Simple stuffed roast peppers

These are so handy because they're great as a vegetarian option or as a side dish with chicken and fish. I love them cold, sliced on lentils or a salad. Or even as a starter, with the option of some fried pancetta on top.

ALL YOU NEED IS

4 red peppers, halved and deseeded

4 large tomatoes

2 garlic cloves, crushed

anchovy fillets, optional
   (1 for each adult's pepper-half)

olive oil

100g goat's cheese

a few fresh basil leaves, torn

ALL YOU DO IS

1. Pre-heat your oven to 180°C (fan), 200°C, gas mark 6 and place the pepper halves on a lightly oiled roasting tray.

2. Then skin the tomatoes by immersing them in a bowl of boiling water for 5 minutes. Remove and, using a tea towel, rub off the skins. (Frankly, I am lazy and often leave the skins on.)

3. Quarter the tomatoes and divide them and the garlic between the pepper halves.

4. If using, roughly chop the anchovies and add 1 fillet per half pepper.

5. Generously dribble olive oil over and into the peppers (about a dessertspoonful each). Bake for 45 minutes in total, but 10 minutes before they come out, crumble in the goat's cheese and torn-up basil leaves.

Babies and kids: *Be careful: they come out of the oven very hot, so let them sit for a bit before little mouths taste them.*

The idiot-proof roast butternut squash soup

This is from my darling friends Neris and India's brilliant book, **Neris and India's Idiot-proof Diet**. The soup is simple, delicious and healthy, and my children love it nearly as much as we love them.

ALL YOU NEED IS

1 large butternut squash, about 1kg (or seasonal pumpkin)

1 tablespoon olive oil

2 tablespoons rosemary leaves

500ml vegetable or organic chicken stock (organic stock cubes are fine)

Parmesan, to serve

ALL YOU DO IS

1. Cut the squash in half lengthways, scoop out the seeds and discard. Drizzle with olive oil, sprinkle with the rosemary and pop into the oven at 180°C (fan), 200°C, gas mark 6 for an 1–1¼ hours, until soft.

2. Scoop out the flesh and rosemary and whizz in a blender. Heat through in a pan with the stock for 20 minutes. (Just add extra stock for the consistency you prefer.)

To serve, sprinkle with grated Parmesan and season your own bowl.

Babies: *Great for the early weaning months.*

Potato dauphinois

A classic French recipe that really is a favourite with everyone. If the cream feels too naughty, replace it with the same amount of milk. It still works really well, just feels less guilty, but as my life is one long guilt trip I tend to serve this with cream as a treat. Great with a roast chicken, lamb or fish.

ALL YOU NEED IS

butter for greasing

2 garlic cloves, crushed

250ml milk

250ml double cream

½ teaspoon ground nutmeg

900g potatoes, very thinly sliced

freshly ground black pepper

180g mature Cheddar, grated

ALL YOU DO IS

1. Rub a little butter around an ovenproof dish (approx. 25 x 25cm), then pre-heat the oven to 180°C (fan), 200°C, gas mark 6.

2. Put the crushed garlic, milk, cream, nutmeg, potatoes and a grind of pepper Into a large saucepan.

3. Bring to the boil, stirring frequently so the potatoes don't stick, and simmer for a couple of minutes to thicken it slightly.

4. Remove from the heat and stir in half the cheese. Empty it all into your oven dish and top with the rest of the cheese. Bake for 45 minutes to 1 hour, until the top is browning and the potatoes are tender.

Babies: *Just mash with a fork.*

Baby carrots with lemon thyme

There are many things in life that depress me. War, cruelty, phone masts, dog poo, flaky fingernails, my mortgage and boiled carrots. I think it's a school-dinner thing. Well, in an effort to take charge of my life, I have discovered that cooking carrots this way can not only cheer me up but leave me wanting more. I am now looking for a recipe for world peace . . .

ALL YOU NEED IS
500ml low-salt vegetable stock
25g butter
juice of ½ lemon
750g baby carrots
a couple of sprigs of lemon thyme

ALL YOU DO IS
1. Bring the stock to the boil. Add the butter and lemon juice. When the butter has melted, add the carrots and cook for 5 or so minutes (to your taste).

2. Using a slotted spoon, take out the carrots and pour some of the liquid out, leaving about 1cm of stock mix in the bottom of the pan. Whack up the heat and reduce. Then pop the carrots back in to coat.

3. Sprinkle with some lemon thyme leaves and try to look on the bright side!

Babies: *Great addition to any meal.*

Serves: **6 adults**   Prep time: **10 minutes**   Cook time: **(including tomato sauce) 15 minutes**

Runner beans in tomato sauce

I admit I'm slightly obsessed with ramming veg down my kids' necks, but this dish is rather tasty and needs only a couple of Chinese burns from me for them to clean their plates.

ALL YOU NEED IS

500g runner beans, sliced diagonally
Italian tomato sauce (p. 175)

ALL YOU DO IS

1.   Boil the beans for 3–4 minutes, then toss in the sauce.

Babies: *Great to pre-cook if you need to, and reheat. Whizz well for the baby in case of stringy bits.*

Nutty pomegranate salad

This is truly a fresh, fruity and unusual salad. Amazing with lamb or fish and it looks so colourful and pretty on the table. When first presented with this, my five-year-old made one of those I'd-rather-eat-my-own-arm faces but I explained that it had all those yummy ingredients that individually she loved. She conceded and polished off her brother's portion too. One point to mummy and about 547,000 to her.

ALL YOU NEED IS

50g plain cashew nuts

2 ripe avocados, diced

1 medium cucumber, diced

¼ red onion, finely chopped

1 pomegranate, seeds only

2 tablespoons fresh chopped coriander

1 tablespoon olive oil

½–1 tablespoon balsamic vinegar

ALL YOU DO IS

1. Pre-heat the oven to 180°C (fan), 200°C, gas mark 6. Toast the nuts on a tray in a medium oven for 15 minutes or until golden, but keep a close eye on them: they can burn easily. When cool, roughly break up in your fingers and put into a bowl along with the avocado, cucumber, onion, pomegranate and coriander.

2. Dress with a good splash of olive oil and a drizzle of balsamic vinegar. Season on your plate.

Kids: *Great for kids old enough to cope with the cashews. Leave out the coriander for younger ones (or my dad) if you think they'll reject it.*

Red rice salad

Very useful, very healthy. As a side dish with chicken or fish, it's great at a barbecue. Or just crumble over some feta cheese for a summer weekday lunch for you.

ALL YOU NEED IS

250g red rice (or brown basmati)

1 stick celery, finely diced

1 carrot, finely diced

3 salad onions, finely chopped

½ small cucumber, diced

10 small cherry tomatoes, halved

1 x 200g tin anchovy-stuffed
   green olives, halved

3 dessertspoons olive oil

1 dessertspoon balsamic vinegar

ALL YOU DO IS

1. Cook the rice as per packet instructions (about 25 minutes). Drain and cool under cold running water.

2. Add all the other ingredients together and dress with the oil and vinegar.

3. Season on your plate.

Babies: *When old enough for rice, I tend to dress theirs with just a drizzle of the oil.*

Roast Parmesan parsnips

I am a parsnip fan. There, now I've said it. Mashed, fried, roasted, whatever. And these are the king of parsnips. I often cook them as an alternative to potatoes. Very little effort for this great side dish.

ALL YOU NEED IS

1kg medium parsnips, peeled
60g pine nuts
80g Parmesan cheese, grated
1 teaspoon dried rosemary
2 tablespoons vegetable oil

ALL YOU DO IS

1. Pre-heat the oven to 180°C (fan), 200°C, gas mark 6. Pre-heat the oil in a large roasting tray.

2. Cut the parsnips into thick chip-width strips, then parboil them for 5 minutes and drain.

3. Meanwhile, chop the pine nuts up a bit, then add to the cheese and rosemary.

4. Toss the parsnips in the cheese mixture and tip into the hot oil.

5. Roast for 45 minutes. Toss them about a bit when you remember.

Babies: *They love these. Great finger food.*

Molto buono beans

I tell the kids this is Italian baked beans. It really has that holiday taste that makes me want to strip off and rub oil all over my body. No wonder it's Dan's favourite. Fabulous with fish and chicken.

ALL YOU NEED IS

2 tablespoons olive oil

2 garlic cloves, crushed

2 x 400g tins cannellini beans, rinsed and drained

1 tablespoon fresh flat-leaf parsley, finely chopped

juice of 1 lemon

2 teaspoons baby capers (optional)

ALL YOU DO IS

1. In a frying pan, heat 1 tablespoon of olive oil, then add the garlic for a minute, followed by the beans. Gently stir until warm, about 3–4 minutes. Take off the heat and throw in the parsley.

2. To serve, dress with another tablespoon of olive oil and the juice of a lemon. Season with black pepper. For the adults, sprinkle over some drained baby capers.

Babies: *Great whizzed up with some fish.*

Tips: *Can be made with tinned borlotti beans, too.*

Warm winter soup

OK, this might seem scary to offer the kids as it is seriously healthy, with cabbage, veg galore and beans. Yes, call the police, children . . . But I have included it because it is so easy and my kids actually like it. So do I! Go on, warm your winter cockles. It's even better the next day.

ALL YOU NEED IS

splash of olive oil

1 onion, finely chopped

2 carrots, finely chopped

2 celery sticks, finely chopped

1 garlic clove, crushed

1 x 400g tin chopped tomatoes

1 tablespoon tomato purée

1 litre low-salt stock (chicken or veg)

2 x 400g tins mixed beans, drained and rinsed

half a Savoy cabbage, finely chopped

ALL YOU DO IS

1. In your oil, gently fry the onion for a minute or two, then add the carrot and celery, followed by the garlic. Soften for 4–5 minutes, covered.

2. Throw in the tomatoes, tomato purée, stock and beans and bring to the boil. Reduce the heat, cover and simmer for another 25 minutes.

3. Stir in the cabbage and continue to simmer for another 10 minutes or until the cabbage is cooked to your taste. I like it still crunchy. Season your own bowl.

Babies: *Whizz it up when they are little.*

Kids and you: *Serve it with crunchy toast, with Parmesan grated on top of theirs and some chopped, fried pancetta on yours.*

Mish-mash

Everyone loves mash. So here are just a few different options to help you think outside of the box. I mush it with a metal hand masher and then often give one or two whizzes with the electric blender. Put your own combos together.

Things to add to your mash:

1. Lemon and chive: lemon juice and grated zest, a good glug of lemon oil and a handful of chopped chives (amazing with fish or chicken).

2. Garlic and butter: gently fry some garlic in butter and add to your mash. Go really crazy and add a touch of cream.

3. Butternut squash: roast your squash and/or sweet potato. Add a good knob of butter and a pinch of nutmeg.

4. Parsnip and horseradish: make your mash from a mixture of potatoes and parsnips in equal measures. Add a good dollop of creamy horseradish, some butter and a tablespoon of crème fraîche.

5. Carrot and coriander: use half carrot and half sweet potato, boiled or roasted, then mashed. Add finely chopped coriander and a splash of olive oil.

6. Chickpea: mash together 2 large boiled potatoes, 2 cans of chickpeas, rinsed and drained, 1 crushed and fried garlic bulb and a splash of olive oil.

Babies, kids and you: *If serving the kids first, reheat later for you. All these freeze for the baby.*

Sexy garlic spinach

Once you've eaten spinach this way, you'll never look back. You can pre-cook it by up to a couple of hours and gently warm through when you're ready. Sometimes Dan asks if he can have something special on a Saturday night. I used to slip into my best lingerie. Now I give him this. He doesn't seem to have noticed the change. Who knew spinach could be so sexy?

ALL YOU NEED IS

900g fresh baby-leaf spinach
75g butter
2 cloves garlic, crushed

ALL YOU DO IS

1. Wash the spinach well, shake dry and cram into a very big pan. Cover with a lid and gently heat through, turning occasionally, for a few minutes.

2. When it has cooked down, remove and drain in a sieve, pushing the water out.

3. Heat the butter and garlic in a saucepan for 1 minute or so. Once the garlic is just turning a light golden, stir in the spinach and heat through.

Babies: *Whizz up in small quantities with the rest of the meal.*

Kids: *Hide it!*

Sweet carrot and lentil soup

Warm, healthy and dead easy to knock up.

ALL YOU NEED IS

1 red onion, finely chopped

1 tablespoon olive oil

400g carrots, roughly chopped

1 stick of celery, roughly chopped

100g red lentils

300g sweet potato, peeled and chopped

800ml organic chicken or low-salt
　vegetable stock

a drizzle of chilli oil

handful of coriander, chopped

ALL YOU DO IS

1. In a large saucepan, fry the onion in olive oil. After a minute or two, add the carrots and celery and pop on a lid.

2. When soft (about 10 minutes), add the lentils, sweet potato and stock. Bring to the boil, then simmer for 20 minutes or so, lid on. Whizz with a hand blender until smooth.

3. Serve the adults' helpings with a swirl of chilli oil and a sprinkle of coriander.

Babies: *A full-on favourite with babies: make loads and freeze.*

Roast garlic and lemon new potatoes

I find new potatoes a little dull and sometimes you just need to mix things up a bit, or life gets rather tedious. A squeeze of something sharp and a quick roasting can do wonders for your spuds. Try it on your partner if things need a shake-up.

ALL YOU NEED IS

750g baby new potatoes, skin on
4 tablespoons olive oil
salt and freshly ground black pepper
2 garlic cloves, crushed
1 lemon, zest and juice

ALL YOU DO IS

1. Pre-heat the oven to 200°C (fan), 220°C, gas mark 7.

2. Throw the washed potatoes into a roasting tray.

3. Drizzle half the oil over the potatoes and toss with a bit of seasoning. Roast for 45–50 minutes, giving them a shake if you remember. Once soft, remove.

4. Mix the garlic with the remaining oil, lemon zest and juice. Spoon this dressing through the hot potatoes and serve immediately.

Garlic bread

Ahhh, the seventies . . . I miss the heady days of the Marie-Rose sauce, cheese fondues and garlic bread. This just replaces the butter overload with olive oil, which feels a bit more twenty-first century but stills hits the spot. Not sure my corkscrew perm will stand the test of time so well.

ALL YOU NEED IS
a long French bread stick
4 garlic cloves, crushed
6 tablespoons olive oil

ALL YOU DO IS
1. Pre-heat the grill to medium high. Cut the bread in half, lengthways down the middle.

2. Lightly toast the underside, then mix the garlic and oil and just drizzle over the inside of the bread.

3. Pop under a hot grill for 4–5 minutes until toasted and golden.

Onion marmalade

This tasty and useful relish is delicious with cheese, quiche, steak sandwich, you name it. In this recipe I have suggested that you serve it with bangers and mash, as it brings a little sophistication to a classic family dish. The marmalade is the grown-up bit, I guess.

ALL YOU NEED IS

6 large onions, thickly sliced into rings
2 tablespoons olive oil
2 tablespoons dark brown sugar
1 tablespoon balsamic vinegar
freshly ground black pepper

ALL YOU DO IS

1. Over a medium heat, in a covered pan, fry your onion slices in the oil until soft and starting to brown, about 20 minutes, stirring every now and then. (Feel free to multi-task.)

2. Then add the sugar, vinegar and a grind of pepper and cook for 5 minutes.

3. Finally add 2 tablespoons of water and cook for a further couple of minutes, uncovered. Cool.

4. Store in a clean, sterilized jar and serve at room temperature with almost anything.

Just pop some organic bangers into the oven and see p. 137 for your favourite mash.

DON'T PANIC

I bet you have more in your fridge and larder than you think. Well, here are a few quick answers for when you are up against it. Which if you are anything like me is every day. I can't remember the last time I was at a loose end.

PS It helps to write lists. I tend to slightly overdo this theory and write lists of the lists I should be following up. However, if you go to the supermarket without one, you tend to over-buy. That's why planning a few days in advance pays off.

PPS Pre-preparing the night before or in the morning can leave you feeling chilled and able to enjoy the cooking experience as opposed to that growing panic bubbling inside as the list of things to get done mounts.

PPPS If you have people coming over, don't leave your appearance till last, as inevitably your guests start to arrive and you look like you have run a mini marathon in a teddy-bear costume. Better that they eat a little late and you greet them with the cool, calm exterior of someone in charge and with clean hair. Otherwise, however good your meringues, all they will remember is your greasy bob.

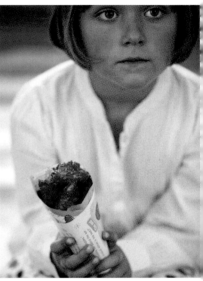

Don't panic

Baked spaghetti carbonara

Quick chicken Kiev

Cheat's tomato and pancetta risotto

Steak sandwich with relish

My normal pasta bake

Sardines on toast and a quick dip

Quick salmon wrap

Mini tuna burgers

Quick salmon and goat's cheese tart

Roasted fish with tomato and olive relish

One-minute mackerel pâté

Mega-quick Italian tomato sauce

Fish popcorns

Warm chicken pesto salad

Quick crusty cod

Creamy Boursin salmon penne

Five-minute mackerel

The mother of all sandwiches

Baked spaghetti carbonara

The crowd will beg for more, I guarantee it . . .

ALL YOU NEED IS

1 small onion, finely chopped

85g pancetta, chopped to bite size

2 garlic cloves, crushed

250g dried spaghetti (about half a packet)

2 large egg yolks

150g asparagus spears

142ml carton single cream

4 tablespoons vegetable stock

5 tablespoons grated Parmesan

4 tablespoons fresh breadcrumbs

1 tablespoon fresh parsley, chopped

1 tablespoon olive oil

ALL YOU DO IS

1. Pre-heat the oven to 180°C (fan), 200°C, gas mark 6. Fry the onion and pancetta, then add the garlic, briefly.

2. Cook the spaghetti, drain and immediately mix the egg yolks with the hot pasta.

3. Steam or blanch the asparagus until just tender but still crunchy (I tend to steam them over the cooking spaghetti).

4. Gently mix together the eggy pasta, the onion and pancetta mixture, asparagus, cream, stock and half of the Parmesan. Pile into an ovenproof dish.

5. Mix together the remaining Parmesan, breadcrumbs, parsley and olive oil and scatter over the top of the pasta. Bake for 15 minutes.

Kids: *My kids just love it. Snip the asparagus into bite-size pieces before putting the dish in the oven.*

Quick chicken Kiev

A quick and easy idea for when you just can't think what to do with those chicken breasts. Cooking them in the parcel keeps everything moist and the flavours and goodness in.

ALL YOU NEED IS

2 (organic) chicken breasts, skin off

1 garlic clove, crushed

1 tablespoon fresh flat-leaf parsley, finely chopped

2 knobs of soft butter (about 40g in total)

6 cherry tomatoes

½ courgette, sliced

3 tablespoons chicken stock

2 sprigs fresh herbs (tarragon, rosemary and thyme all work well)

ALL YOU DO IS

1. Pre-heat the oven to 180°C (fan), 200°C, gas mark 6.

2. Cut lengthways along the top of the chicken breasts, about halfway down, to make a pocket. Place the breasts on a large piece of foil, pulling up the sides to make a boat shape.

3. Now mix the garlic, parsley and butter together and divide between the two breasts, filling the pockets.

4. Dot the tomatoes and courgettes in the boat as well, then pour over the stock and finally pop your sprigs of fresh herbs on top.

5. Put another piece of foil on top as a lid and scrunch to seal. Cook for 30–35 minutes or until cooked through.

Serve with crispy roast potatoes and a green salad. Season on your plate.

Babies: *Also great whizzed with mash for little ones.*

Cheat's tomato and pancetta risotto

The joy of this rice dish is that you don't have to hover over it like other risottos. I often pop some seared tuna on top. Easy-peasy everyday classic.

ALL YOU NEED IS

1 onion, finely chopped

50g pancetta, chopped

25g butter

splash of olive oil

250g risotto rice

850ml chicken stock

250ml tomato passata

2 tablespoons Parmesan, grated

ALL YOU DO IS

1. In a saucepan, soften the onion and cook the pancetta in the butter and oil. Add the rice and stir for a minute or so.

2. Turn up the heat and add the stock and passata. Bring to the boil. Stir once, then turn down the heat to a simmer and leave with a lid on for 15–20 minutes. Let it sit for 5 minutes before serving.

Grate over some Parmesan and season on your plate.

Babies: *A winner for the little ones. The soft rice makes a perfect first rice experience.*

Kids: *I like to serve the kids' portions with garden peas cooked and mixed through the rice at the last minute. And a green salad for us.*

Steak sandwich with relish

This seems to really fit the bill on a Saturday lunch-time after football, swimming and all things sweaty. Great hangover food for you.

ALL YOU NEED IS

For the relish:

1 avocado, roughly mashed

2 tomatoes, deseeded and chopped

1 tablespoon lime juice

1 tablespoon coriander, chopped

4 thin steaks

1 long French loaf or similar

4 big soft lettuce leaves

ALL YOU DO IS

1. To make the relish, just mix all the ingredients in a bowl.

2. Then, in a splash of oil, fry the steak on a high heat for about a minute each side (better still, whack it on the barbecue).

3. Pop a lettuce leaf Into some French bread, lay the steak on top and spoon on the relish.

Babies and kids: *Serve with ketchup for the kids, of course! You can whizz or chop the steak for the baby by adding some avocado relish and perhaps a drop of olive oil.*

Sardines on toast and a quick dip

This is great as a super-quick light lunch or tea for the kids, or a snack on the run for all the family. Good for them, good for you, not so good for the sardine, but hey, something's got to give.

ALL YOU NEED IS

1 ripe avocado

1 x 200g tub houmous

1 x 120g tin sardines in olive oil

a pile of toast

butter

freshly ground black pepper

squeeze of lemon

a selection of your favourite raw veg
   (carrot, cucumber, tomatoes,
   peppers, etc.)

a few chopped coriander leaves

half a fresh red chilli, finely chopped

ALL YOU DO IS

1. Mash the avocado with a fork and mix it with the houmous. Spoon it into little pots or egg cups.

2. Divide the sardines on to lightly buttered toast. Grind over a little pepper and give them a squeeze of lemon. Cut into fingers or triangles.

3. Chop your veg and arrange with the fish fingers and dip pots on a plate. Serve.

Babies: *Great finger food. (Lightly boil the carrots if too hard.)*

You: *For the adults' dip, mix in the coriander and chilli.*

Quick salmon wrap

Super-quick, this is my standby when I have no time and can't think what to cook. I tend to wrap Parker's in just the ham and Sonny's I leave plain. A great quick panic dinner-party recipe when you have just got back from work and your guests are arriving in ten minutes.

ALL YOU NEED IS

4 salmon fillets, about 150g each

olive oil

80g goat's cheese

4 large basil leaves

4 slices Black Forest or Parma ham

ALL YOU DO IS

1. Pre-heat the oven to 200°C (fan), 220°C, gas mark 7 and lightly oil a roasting tray. Put the fillets on the tray.

2. Place a knob of goat's cheese and a basil leaf on top of the adults' fish fillets.

3. Then take one piece of the ham per fillet and place on top of the lot. Tuck the ends under.

4. Roast for 10–15 minutes (a bit longer for the kids).

Serve with red rice salad (p. 129) in summer and whole sweet potatoes roasted in their jackets in winter. Season on your plate.

Babies: *They love the smooth, mild taste of salmon.*

Mini tuna burgers

You can make and cook these in a matter of minutes. A healthy, fresh alternative to the usual burger options. Fun for when the kids' friends are over, and rather tasty for you, too.

ALL YOU NEED IS

2 fresh tuna steaks (approx. 250g)

2 salad onions, roughly chopped

1 tablespoon fresh coriander, finely chopped

1 tablespoon sesame seeds

1 small lime

1 tablespoon olive oil

12 slices of bread or 6 mini buns (warmed or toasted)

ALL YOU DO IS

1. Roughly cut up the tuna and pop it into a food processor with the salad onions and coriander. Pulse until roughly minced. Add the sesame seeds and a good squeeze of lime juice and mix together.

2. With damp hands, shape into 6 burgers. Refrigerate till needed.

3. When ready, just fry them in a little olive oil for a minute or so on each side or until just cooked through for kids. I like mine pink in the middle.

4. If you don't have the mini buns, use a round biscuit cutter to cut out 12 circles from the middle of the slices of bread and lightly toast them.

Serve with lots of fresh raw veg and a dollop of houmous or mayo for the kids.

Babies: *Great finger food, freeze them raw.*

You: *Yours can be served without the bun on a fresh green salad dressed with lemon and oil, if you prefer. Try adding a teaspoon of wasabi paste to your mayo!*

Quick salmon and goat's cheese tart

This is Parker's favourite, and the combo would work well on a pizza base too. Good for a picnic. Or if friends are over, make one big one and serve with salad. Again, if someone asks, 'Is this your pastry?' answer, 'Yes.' After all, it is. You bought it.

ALL YOU NEED IS

375g pack ready-rolled puff pastry sheet
4 large tomatoes, thinly sliced
100g French goat's cheese
300g sliced smoked salmon
handful of chopped chives

ALL YOU DO IS

1. Pre-heat the oven to 180°C (fan), 200°C, gas mark 6.

2. Line a roasting tray with baking paper. Unroll 'your' pastry on to the tray and cut to your preferred shape.

3. Scatter on the slices of tomato, then crumble the cheese over and finally arrange the salmon on top.

4. Pop in the oven, on the top shelf, for approximately 10–15 minutes for the individual tarts, 25–30 for the big one, or until the pastry is golden. Use the paper to help you slide the tart on to a big wooden board.

5. To serve, just sprinkle with chopped chives.

Babies: *Full-on finger food.*

Roasted fish with tomato and olive relish

This is one of the simplest recipes in the book and, dare I say, one of the tastiest. It is inspired by my mother-in-law's larder, which is packed with jars and packets of Italian goodies. She can whip up a meal when there is seemingly nothing in the house just by opening that magic cupboard. Mind you, she does live on a remote Tuscan hillside with her own olive grove. If you don't grow your own olives, dry your own tomatoes or pickle your own capers, then perhaps just buy them from the corner shop.

ALL YOU NEED IS

4 skinless white fish fillets
   (cod, haddock, etc.), about 175g each

For the relish:

100g pitted black olives

100g sun-blushed tomatoes and
   2 tablespoons of their oil from the jar

1 tablespoon capers, drained

half a 50g tin of anchovies

2 garlic cloves, peeled

25g fresh basil

ALL YOU DO IS

1. Pre-heat the oven to 180°C (fan), 200°C , gas mark 6.

2. Pulse all of the ingredients for the relish in a food processor. Don't go crazy, as you want it to be quite coarse – like it's been chopped.

3. When you are ready to roast, just lay the fish on a lightly oiled baking tray and, for those that want it, give each of the fish fillets a heaped spoonful of relish spread over the top.

4. Bake for approximately 20 minutes, depending on the thickness of your fish.

Great served with chive and lemon mash (p. 137).

Babies and kids: I tend to just roast the younger kids' fish without any relish. The oils and garlic from ours infuse theirs. Try adding just a little to the older ones' portions and say it's like a pizza topping. Works for me!

171 Don't panic

One-minute mackerel pâté

This is great for lunch, snacks, picnics, parties, lunch boxes and teatime dips. It's made in a minute, literally, and couldn't be tastier or, God forbid, healthier. It's Parker's favourite after-school snack.

ALL YOU NEED IS
1 x 200g pack smoked mackerel
2 tablespoons low-fat cottage cheese
1 tablespoon half-fat crème fraîche
juice of 1 lemon
pepper to taste
horseradish (for you)

ALL YOU DO IS
1. Bung it all in a food processor and pulse.

(I tend to remove one of the skins and leave the other on for the oily good stuff.)

Babies: *Love it on toast.*

You: *For an extra kick, add a teaspoon of horseradish.*

Mega-quick Italian tomato sauce

I sometimes use this tomato sauce for the meatballs on page 44, but it's so handy as a base for loads of different dishes. Use on pasta or pizza and over fish, sausages, roasted veg, rice, chick peas, all sorts.

ALL YOU NEED IS

1 large onion, chopped

1 tablespoon olive oil

2–3 garlic cloves, crushed

700g bottle of tomato passata

2 teaspoons balsamic vinegar

ALL YOU DO IS

1. Fry the onion in the oil until soft (10 minutes-ish), then add the garlic to colour very slightly.

2. Pour in the passata and vinegar and heat through for another 5 minutes or so.

Fish popcorns

These little nuggets of crispy fish are a sure-fire weekday winner with all ages. You can make them up earlier in the day if you need to and keep them in the fridge. Definitely one of Sonny's favourites.

ALL YOU NEED IS

1 large egg

4 handfuls of cornflakes
   (no salt/sugar ones if possible)

3 tablespoons plain or spelt flour

250g skinned white fish fillets
   (haddock works well)

1 tablespoon olive oil

ALL YOU DO IS

1. In a bowl, beat the egg. In a bag, with your hands, crush the cornflakes into rough crumbs and transfer to another bowl. Put the flour into a third bowl.

2. Chop the fish into small bite-size pieces.

3. First coat the fish in the flour, then dip in the beaten egg and lastly transfer to the crumbs and toss to coat. Tip on to a lightly greased baking tray.

4. When ready, pre-heat the oven to 180°C (fan), 200°C, gas mark 6. Drizzle with the oil and roast for 15–20 minutes till crispy.

Babies: *Magic finger food.*

Warm chicken pesto salad

This is about throwing all the ingredients together, and the combo really is tasty. A great summer lunch or after-school dinner that can be prepared beforehand if you need to.

ALL YOU NEED IS

500g new potatoes, skin on

3 x 125g organic chicken breasts, skinned and cubed

2 tablespoons olive oil, plus a little for frying

juice of 1 lemon

2 tablespoons fresh pesto (buy it at the deli section)

100g watercress, washed

ALL YOU DO IS

1. Chop the potatoes in half and boil until they are tender and fall off a fork. Drain. Then, with the curve of a spoon, roughly break them up and put in a big bowl.

2. Meanwhile, stir-fry the chicken in a little oil for about 8–10 minutes on a medium-high heat. When cooked through and golden, add to the potatoes.

3. Dress the lot with the lemon juice, pesto and olive oil. Roughly chop up the watercress and also throw into the bowl. Toss. Eat. Yum.

Babies: *I just whizz it all with a couple of sprigs of watercress only and a drop of boiled water.*

Kids: *Don't overdo their watercress. It might scare them.*

Quick crusty cod

The great thing about this quick-fix recipe is that you can vary what you add to your breadcrumbs. Chopped tomatoes or fried mushrooms, Parmesan or feta, it will all work. The pesto option I have picked because the kids love it . . .

ALL YOU NEED IS

2 heaped tablespoons breadcrumbs (whizz up any old bread-bin leftovers)

1 tablespoon fresh thyme leaves, chopped

1 tablespoon olive oil

2 x 150g cod (or pretty much any fish) fillets, skinless and boneless

2 heaped teaspoons fresh pesto

ALL YOU DO IS

1. Pre-heat the oven to 180°C (fan), 200°C, gas mark 6. Mix the breadcrumbs and fresh thyme with the olive oil.

2. Pop the fillets on a lightly oiled roasting tray. Spread a teaspoon of the pesto on top of each fillet. Then divide the herby breadcrumb mix between the 2 fillets, pressing down lightly on top.

3. Bake for 15–20 minutes until the fish is cooked through.

Serve with some roasted tomatoes and sexy spinach (p. 138).

You: *Try swapping the pesto for horseradish.*

Creamy Boursin salmon penne

This is guaranteed to be tasty and quick. Parker has been known to lick the sauce clean off the plate. If she did that when she was out, I would, of course, be furious, but at home I can't help seeing it as a triumph. So many mixed messages, poor kid.

ALL YOU NEED IS

300g penne

1 big head of broccoli,
  cut into small florets

2 salmon fillets, skinned and cubed
  (150g each)

200ml Greek yogurt

150g pack Boursin soft garlic cheese

2 dessertspoons tomato purée

a few basil leaves

ALL YOU DO IS

1. Cook the pasta, adding the broccoli a couple of minutes before it is ready, then drain. If you have a steamer that will fit on top of the pan, then steam the fish over the pasta. If not, use a colander with a lid on. It should only take 5 minutes or so.

2. Meanwhile mix the yogurt, Boursin and tomato purée. Then gently mix the cooked pasta, salmon and the sauce together. Dress with a few basil leaves and serve.

Babies: *Chop up small. They love it.*

Tip: *Oil the steamer or colander a little so the fish doesn't stick.*

Five-minute mackerel

When I first tried giving the family fresh mackerel, I thought I was going to have a revolution on my hands. Surely something that healthy would be rejected at the first suspicious mouthful? But a minor miracle occurred when 'OOooo's and 'AAaaa's came floating across my kitchen table. I was so pleased that I served it every day for a week until they all begged for mackerel mercy. As a result, we have had to take a short break from our fishy friend, but be warned: it will be back. Its crispy outside and soft, creamy flesh are addictive.

ALL YOU NEED IS

4 x 80g fresh mackerel fillets, boned
  (2 x 80g fillets per adult, 1 for a child)

a plate of plain or white spelt flour or
  semolina flour (approx. 50g)

a knob of butter

1 lemon

ALL YOU DO IS

1. Double-check for bones by running a finger over the fish fillets, and remove them: tweezers work well.

2. Coat the fillets on both sides in flour.

3. Fry them on a high-ish heat in a knob of butter for 2–3 minutes each side.

4. Squeeze over the lemon juice.

Serve with lemon and chive mash (p. 137) or rice and some lovely purple sprouting broccoli.

Babies: *Just break it up with your fingers and chuck away the skin, which gives you a chance to double-check for bones.*

Tip: *Ask your fishmonger (including those in supermarkets) to pin-bone your mackerel.*

The mother of all sandwiches

Put this on your picnic blanket and just lap up the applause. Add or take away ingredients to make your favourite combo. Make it the day before. A crowd pleaser.

ALL YOU NEED IS

1 large, round rustic loaf (pain de campagne or similar)

200g pesto (fresh is best here)

2 tablespoons olive oil

1 tablespoon balsamic vinegar

150g sliced (organic) chicken

2 large ripe tomatoes, sliced

2 x 120g balls of mozzarella, drained and sliced

75g salami or ham

handful of fresh, washed young leaf spinach

ALL YOU DO IS

1. Cut a lid off the top of the loaf and set aside.

2. Gouge out the inside of the loaf, leaving a hollow shell, then bung the bread from inside in a food processor and pulse into breadcrumbs. Split in half and mix one half with the pesto and the other half with a dressing of the oil and vinegar.

3. Now assemble in layers starting with the pesto crumbs, then chicken, then tomato, then mozzarella, then salami or ham, then spinach, then the dressed breadcrumbs. Push down each layer really well with the back of a large spoon each time.

4. When it is all evenly packed in, pop on the lid, wrap tightly in cling film and leave overnight in the fridge with something heavy on top.

To serve, slice like a cake.

DON'T PANIC PUDDINGS

A good chocolate sauce over ice-cream and fruit can be the best pudding ever. Frankly, it's all about the presentation. You can get away with next to no effort if you pile it on a pretty plate or into a glass. A sprig of mint or grating of chocolate, perhaps?

Sometimes, after a big meal, the simplest of puddings works best.

Don't panic puddings

Cheat's jam tarts

Chocolate fondue

Roasted peaches and ice-cream

Chocolate affogato

Emergency frozen yogurt

Rushed roast bananas

Custard lollies

Cheat's jam tarts

A quick fix for parties and, as I keep saying, it's your pastry. You bought it.

ALL YOU NEED IS

375g pack sweet shortcrust pastry

75g raspberry jam
  (seedless if possible, but not essential)

75g apricot jam

2 x 12-hole non-stick tart tins

ALL YOU DO IS

1. Heat the oven to 200°C (fan), 220°C, gas mark 7.

2. Roll out the pastry and cut circles a little bigger than each hole, 8cm-ish.

3. Overlapping the edge a little, place the rounds in the tins.

4. Then add a teaspoon of jam per tart and bake for 10–15 minutes, or until the jam bubbles and the pastry is cooked.

5. Allow to cool a little in the tin.

Tip: *I use a 'no added sugar' jam, but you can use up any jam you have lying around. Even Nutella works.*

Tip: *If you only have one tin, just bake in batches.*

Chocolate fondue

This is a brilliant solution for a hot summer lunch with friends and family. Great for a barbie. It's fun, messy and you don't have to have a fondue set to have a go.

ALL YOU NEED IS

300g Toblerone

300g dark chocolate

100ml double cream

a few fresh mint leaves to decorate

Chopped fruit – fruit that works well includes pear, banana, pineapple, mango, strawberries, all berries really, cherries, kiwis, oranges, grapes, peaches

ALL YOU DO IS

1. In a heatproof bowl over gently simmering water, melt all the chocolate.

2. Add the cream and gently heat through. So that it stays runny, place the heatproof bowl inside another, larger ceramic bowl that you can put on the table. Pour some hot water in between the bowls.

Serve immediately with piles of chopped fruit and some wet wipes close by.

Roasted peaches and ice-cream

A mega-quick pudding that rocks . . .

ALL YOU NEED IS

4 ripe peaches, washed,
   halved and stoned

4 teaspoons dark brown sugar

4 tablespoons toasted flaked almonds

good-quality vanilla ice-cream

ALL YOU DO IS

1. Heat the oven to 200°C (fan), 220°C, gas mark 7. Pop the halved peaches on a roasting tray. Sprinkle over the sugar and almonds. Heat through for 15 minutes.

2. Serve hot, with a dollop of ice-cream on top.

Babies: *I like to roast a peach plain for the very small ones and mush into some Greek yogurt.*

Chocolate affogato

Affogato means 'drowned' in Italian. This classic recipe is simply vanilla ice-cream drowned in coffee, which in itself is delicious and a brilliant quick-fix pudding. The Toblerone sauce poured on top was originally intended to appeal to the kids, but it was such a hit, especially with Giorgio, my Italian father-in-law, that I have to call this one a Fay's Family Favourite.

ALL YOU NEED IS

For the sauce:

200g Toblerone

50ml double cream

500g tub of good-quality vanilla ice-cream

300ml pot of hot black coffee, espresso if possible

ALL YOU DO IS

1. Break up the chocolate (trying not to eat it all) and melt it in a bowl over simmering water, adding the cream and mixing together over a gentle heat till smooth.

2. In a glass or coffee cup put a couple of scoops of ice-cream followed by the chocolate sauce.

3. For the adults, pour an espresso-sized shot of coffee over the chocolate sauce and ice-cream. Eat immediately.

Emergency frozen yogurt

Some days, nothing goes your way. I discovered this emergency treat on just such a day, when the washing machine was leaking, the goldfish had died (again) and my daughter decided she would whinge until ice-cream was put in her mouth. Well, it worked. Parker's face finally cracked a smile, she forgot about the fish and I used the empty yogurt carton to catch the drips from the washing machine. Job done . . .

Stock up on frozen berries. They're a life saver.

ALL YOU NEED IS
4 tablespoons Greek yogurt
2 handfuls of frozen berries (approx. 75g)
1 dessertspoon runny honey
1 banana, peeled
chocolate Flake (optional)

ALL YOU DO IS
1. Whizz everything except the Flake in a food processor until thick, smooth and combined.

2. Serve immediately, in a tall glass. Stick a chocolate Flake in yours, obviously.

A great pudding for everyone. You can also spoon into ice-lolly moulds and freeze.

Rushed roast bananas

I reckon cooked fruit is a bit of a rip-off as puddings go, but this is gorgeous and the hot–cold, sweet–sharp combo really works. You can up the naughtiness factor by serving it with ice-cream. Don't be put off by the fact that it looks like a drowned man's penis – it's a great midweek dessert.

ALL YOU NEED IS

2 bananas, peeled

a squeeze of lemon juice

2 tablespoons freshly squeezed
   orange juice

2 tablespoons runny honey (approx.)

1 ripe passion fruit

2 tablespoons Greek yogurt or vanilla
   ice-cream

ALL YOU DO IS

1. Pre-heat the oven to 200°C (fan), 220°C, gas mark 7.

2. Wrap each banana in foil, leaving the parcel open at the top. Give each a squeeze of lemon, a tablespoon of orange juice, about a tablespoon of honey and finally scrape half a passion fruit in.

3. Seal up the parcels and bake on a tray for about 15–20 minutes.

Serve with vanilla ice-cream and any berries you have lying around.

Custard lollies

Apparently the idea of freezing custard came after the war as a replacement for ice-cream. Then, they used the powdered stuff. Now, I use any posh ready-made vanilla custard. The end result is smooth, creamy and the best lolly money can buy. It's my pudding of choice and I genuinely resent the kids eating them (which I accept is wrong) . . .

ALL YOU NEED IS

500g tub of fresh ready-made
  vanilla custard

ALL YOU DO IS

1. Pour the custard into some lolly moulds and freeze.

IT'S MY PARTY AND I'LL EAT SUGAR IF I WANT TO

When I was a child, my dad rationed my sugar intake in case he ended up with a fat daughter, which for him was not on the menu. So of course I would sneak downstairs in the dead of night and, secret squirrel, stuff my face with cookies till I burst. Durr! Dad, what did you expect?

As a result, I swore that when I grew up any kid of mine would have a Cadbury's credit card and a guilt-free ride on any sugar high they wanted. But guess what went and happened . . . ?

The minute I pushed a little human being out of my body, I started rationing sugar like it was 1940. Poor little Parker got really excited about organic raisins and carrot sticks until she was well into her third year of life. Then finally I realized it was time to take a sugar chill pill when I allowed her a long-awaited first ice-cream cone. She stared at it for a moment, then asked me, 'Why is the microphone melting?'

Now I have found a happy medium, I hope. My kids have treats but they are exactly that. Treats. I don't add sugar to the baby's food and do try to delay their sweet tooth for as long as it seems humane.

My dad, ironically, has now become 'the lollipop man', trading in illicit sweetie supplies to my kids. I, however, am still sneaking off in the dead of night to the cookie jar.

It's my party and I'll eat sugar if I want to

Chocolate and pear upside-down cake

Lemon shortbreads

Mini meringues with raspberry cream

Creamy lemon pots

Grown-up jammy dodgers

Lemon drizzle cake

Raspberry sweethearts

Killer cupcakes

Quick chocolate torte

Lime cheesecake with a chocolate crunch

Break-your-diet brownies

'Good afternoon' apple cake

My mum's apple and blackberry crumble

I-promise-it's-easy pavlova

Party jelly boats

Chocolate and pear upside-down cake

Yum, bloody yum. Well, there were four of us and no leftovers. Admittedly we were all meant to be on diets, so there was an element of mania in the air, but I reckon even Posh Spice would have seconds of this mega chocolate–pear combo.

ALL YOU NEED IS

35g butter

250g light brown sugar

4 ripe pears, peeled, cored and thickly sliced

150g plain chocolate

180g white spelt or plain flour

40g cocoa powder

¼ teaspoon bicarbonate of soda

1 teaspoon baking powder

2 large eggs

200ml buttermilk or soured cream

75ml vegetable oil

ALL YOU DO IS

1. Melt the butter in a 20–25cm ovenproof frying pan (non-stick is good).

2. Stir in half the sugar and heat for a couple of minutes, stirring continuously until it becomes a light caramel colour.

3. Take off the heat and scatter in the sliced pears. Then break the chocolate into bite-sized pieces and dot amongst the pear. Set aside.

4. In a bowl, sift the flour, cocoa, bicarbonate and baking powder.

5. In a jug or bowl, whisk the eggs, the remaining sugar, buttermilk and oil. Then pour this into the flour mixture and combine to form a batter. Pop into the fridge till needed. (I tend to pre-prepare up until this point.)

6. When ready, pre-heat the oven to 180°C (fan), 200°C, gas mark 6. Pour the batter into the frying pan over the pears and chocolate, spreading it out to the sides of the pan, and bake for 30 minutes. Stand for 5 minutes.

7. Then, being very careful not to burn yourself, place a big plate over the hot pan and flip, turning your cake upside-down.

Serve with loads of whipped cream.

Lemon shortbreads

These little lemon biscuits are delicious and so useful. They store and freeze really well. And they're quick and easy to make. Serve with a dollop of crème fraîche and a berry or two on top, or serve alongside ice-cream, yogurt or mousse. Fill a jam jar with them and wrap a ribbon around the top if you are visiting a friend. Try not to look smug as you hand them over . . .

ALL YOU NEED IS

175g soft butter
Don't forget: take the butter out of the fridge
90g caster sugar
zest of 1 unwaxed lemon, finely grated

1 large egg yolk
250g plain or white spelt flour, sifted
1 large egg, beaten
granulated sugar, to sprinkle

ALL YOU DO IS

1. Cream the butter, sugar and lemon zest till light and fluffy-ish (with an electric whisk, of course!).

2. Add the egg yolk and combine gently. Then gradually (I must emphasize *gradually*) whisk in the flour until it comes together into a dough. I use my hands towards the end: it's easier. Wrap in cling film and pop into the fridge for half an hour (or into the freezer for another day).

3. Pre-heat the oven to 180°C (fan), 200°C, gas mark 6.

4. When it has firmed up just a little, roll out the dough to 5mm-ish thickness. (I find it less stressful to roll half at a time.) Don't use too much extra flour doing this. Using the top of a jar or a round cutter, cut out your biscuit shapes.

5. Using a wide knife or spatula, scoop them up and place them on lined baking sheets and brush with the beaten egg. Sprinkle with sugar and bake for 10 minutes or until golden.

Tip: *Make well in advance for kids' parties. Why? Because you can.*

Mini meringues with raspberry cream

Anyone can make these, I promise. They are so pretty for a party or special tea, or frankly just because you want them. Each one is a mouthful of deliciousness.

ALL YOU NEED IS

2 large egg whites

1 teaspoon white vinegar

150g caster sugar

2 teaspoons icing sugar, sieved

160ml double cream

125g raspberries

ALL YOU DO IS

1. Pre-heat the oven to 120°C (fan), 140°C, gas mark 1. Line 2 large roasting trays with baking paper.

2. Whisk the egg whites (using an electric whisk) with the vinegar and caster sugar, until it is thick and glossy. This should take about 4 minutes. Now fold in the icing sugar with a metal spoon.

3. With a teaspoon, drop a blob of the mixture at a time on to the trays, leaving a small space between them. Bake for 45 minutes in the middle or lower oven. Take out and cool. Peel them gently off the paper.

4. When ready, whisk the cream until thick enough to spread. Add the raspberries and beat them in with a fork so that they colour the cream to a rich girlie pink.

5. Use a knife to spread on the cream and sandwich the two halves together.

Storage: *Make the shells a few days in advance and keep in an airtight box.*

Creamy lemon pots

I fight the kids for these. If they so much as take a breath between bites, I demolish theirs as well as mine. They are basically lemon tarts without the heaviness of the pastry. Many times I have been caught sucking the custard out of a citrus tart. Not a pretty sight.

These are moreish, easy and quick. You can make them in the morning and keep them in the fridge. Definitely good enough for a dinner party, too.

ALL YOU NEED IS

4 large eggs

150g caster sugar

grated zest of 2 unwaxed lemons

120ml lemon juice

120ml single cream

whipping cream to serve

4 ramekins

ALL YOU DO IS

1. Pre-heat your oven to 160°C (fan), 180°C, gas mark 4.

2. Whisk the eggs and sugar till smooth (use an electric whisk if you can). Add the lemon zest and juice. Lastly, whisk the single cream in quickly.

3. Pour the mixture into the ramekins. Place them in a roasting tray. Move it to the oven and pour in boiled water to two-thirds of the way up the sides of the ramekins.

4. Bake for 20–25 minutes until just set. Remove, cool and pop in the fridge until you need them.

5. To serve, whisk the whipping cream and plop a spoonful on top of your delicious little puddings.

Grown-up jammy dodgers

Like so many things from our childhood, the memory of it is so much better than the real thing. Donny Osmond being the exception to the rule. When I finally met him after years of devotion, he was just as sweet as I imagined. Although he didn't seem to be as in love with me as I had hoped. However, jammy dodgers definitely need reinventing and these are melt-in-the-mouth good.

ALL YOU NEED IS

275g white spelt or plain flour

175g caster sugar

275g butter, softened
Don't forget: take the butter out of the fridge

175g ground almonds

½ teaspoon ground cinnamon

3–4 teaspoons raspberry jam

3–4 teaspoons apricot jam

1 tablespoon icing sugar

ALL YOU DO IS

1. With an electric whisk, beat the flour, sugar, butter, almonds and cinnamon into a dough. Get your hands in there if it looks a bit like crumble and bring it together into a ball. Pop into the fridge for half an hour to firm up.

2. Line 2 roasting trays with baking paper.

3. When ready, pre-heat the oven to 180°C (fan), 200°C, gas mark 6. Using plenty of flour, roll out the pastry to 5mm-ish thick. I tend to roll out half at a time. Then, with an 8cm round cutter, cut out your shapes and lay out on the trays. Using a small round bottle top (3cm) or similar, make a hole in the centre of half of them.

4. Bake for 15 minutes and, whilst still hot, spoon half a teaspoon of jam into the middle of the whole biscuits.

5. When cool, place the other half on top and dust with icing sugar.

Serve with your feet up, listening to a pop idol of your choice.

Lemon drizzle cake

The first cake I ever made was a version of this one. It was at school and I remember thinking I must be a genius to produce something so delicious. I went on to fail most exams, but clung to that brief moment of success. Some people have a First from Oxford, others a Lemon Drizzle . . .

ALL YOU NEED IS

200g soft butter
   Don't forget: take the butter out of the fridge
200g golden caster sugar
3 large organic eggs
50g plain or white spelt flour
125g ground almonds
zest of 2 lemons, finely grated
juice of 1 lemon

For the icing:
juice of 1 lemon
5–6 tablespoons icing sugar

a 20–22cm round cake tin

ALL YOU DO IS

1. Pre-heat your oven to 180°C (fan), 200°C, gas mark 6. Line (at least the bottom of) a round cake tin (20–22cm). Butter the sides.

2. Cream together the butter and sugar until light and fluffy (again, don't stress: I use an electric hand whisk).

3. Slowly whisk in the eggs one at a time, then slowly add the flour and finally the almonds and lemon zest. (Hang on to the juice.)

4. Plop the mixture into your tin and bake for 35–40 minutes. Remove from the oven and – whilst still hot and still in the tin – stab with a chopstick or some such weapon all over the cake: 15 or so holes. (Think GBH, not murder.) Drizzle the juice of 1 lemon into the holes and all over the cake. Leave in the tin to cool.

5. To make the icing, just mix a little lemon juice at a time into the icing sugar to make a light paste. Smooth it on to the top of the cake. If it is too thick, just add more juice and vice versa.

This is brilliant to make a day or two before, or freeze. Add the icing on the day.

Raspberry sweethearts

These are called friands and I first discovered them in Australia. Over there, they are as common as the fairy cake except altogether more delicate. Dusted with icing sugar they are a thing of beauty and nice and easy to make.

ALL YOU NEED IS

115g unsalted butter

30g plain or white spelt flour

130g icing sugar, plus extra for dusting

100g ground almonds

3 large egg whites

grated zest of 1½ unwaxed lemons

100g fresh or frozen raspberries

ALL YOU DO IS

1. Heat your oven to 180°C (fan), 200°C, gas mark 6.

2. Melt the butter and use a little of it to generously grease a 6-hole muffin tin. (I use a heart-shaped muffin tin for extra show-off value.)

3. Separately sift the flour and icing sugar into a bowl. Add the almonds and mix.

4. Whisk the egg whites in another bowl to soft-peak stage. Then tip the eggs into the flour mix. Add the zest. Pour in the butter and gently fold the whole lot together, using a big metal spoon.

5. When combined, pour into the tins. Then drop 2 or 3 raspberries on to each cake.

6. Bake for 20–25 minutes. Cool in the tins for 10 minutes, then turn out and leave to cool.

To serve, dust with icing sugar.

Storage: *These keep really well for up to 2 days in an airtight container.*

Killer cupcakes

These little darlings are quick, easy and so pretty. Both flavours are worth making.

ALL YOU NEED IS

150g caster sugar

85g butter, soft
  Don't forget: take the butter out of the fridge

2 large eggs, beaten

220g plain or white spelt flour

1 teaspoon baking powder

150ml milk

2 tablespoons cocoa powder

zest and juice of 1 small lemon

For the toppings:

300g half-fat cream cheese

150g icing sugar

100g dark chocolate, melted

zest and juice of 1 small lemon

paper muffin cups

ALL YOU DO IS

1. Pre-heat your oven to 180°C (fan), 200°C, gas mark 6 and line a 12-hole muffin tin with muffin cases.

2. Whisk the sugar and soft butter until light and fluffy-ish. Slowly whisk in the eggs.

3. Sift in the flour and baking powder. Add the milk and, without over-mixing, combine until smooth.

4. OK, now put half the mixture into a separate bowl. Sift the cocoa powder into one bowl and fold to combine. Into the other, grate the zest of one lemon and add its juice. Gently combine.

5. Fill half the cases with lemon mix and half with choc. Bake for 15–20 minutes.

6. Whilst they're cooling, make the toppings. In a bowl, mix the cream cheese and icing sugar. Separate half into another bowl. Add melted chocolate to one, and the zest and only a dessertspoon of juice to the other. Decorate the lemon ones with the lemon topping and the chocolate cakes with the choc topping.

Tip: *You can freeze the cakes and add the topping when defrosted to room temperature. Or make the cake part the day before and add the topping on the day.*

Quick chocolate torte

Smooth, chocolatey, quick, easy and delicious. This one is a great fall-back pudding that anyone can manage. (It's wheat-free too, if you care.) It needs dressing up a bit before serving, as it is a little 'rustic'-looking. (I know the feeling.) A dusting of cocoa or icing sugar should do the trick.

ALL YOU NEED IS

200g butter, cubed

200g dark chocolate, broken up

6 large eggs, separated

200g caster sugar

cocoa powder for dusting

a 24cm loose-bottomed cake tin

ALL YOU DO IS

1. Heat the oven to 180°C (fan), 200°C, gas mark 6. Grease the sides of the tin and line the base with baking parchment.

2. Melt the butter and chocolate in a glass or metal bowl over gently bubbling water. Leave to cool.

3. Beat the egg yolks and sugar together for a couple of minutes until smooth, then add to your chocolate mix. Combine.

4. Beat the egg whites to stiff peaks and place half into your chocolate/egg mix. Fold gently till combined, then do the same with the remaining egg whites.

5. Pour into your tin and bake in the middle of the oven on a baking tray for 45 minutes or until the centre of the cake feels just set.

6. Leave it to cool. (It will sink down, but don't panic.) When cool, run a knife around the sides and turn out.

Before serving, dust with cocoa. Great with berries and thick whipped cream.

Storing: *It keeps well in an airtight container for up to 3 days.*

Lime cheesecake with a chocolate crunch

To die for . . .

ALL YOU NEED IS

40g butter

20g dark chocolate

50g ground almonds

100g dark chocolate digestive biscuits or similar, crushed

800g light cream cheese

185g soured cream

175g caster sugar

4 large eggs and 2 large egg whites

zest of 3 limes

1½ tablespoons lime juice

ALL YOU DO IS

1. Line the base of a loose-bottomed cake tin (24cm) with baking paper.

2. Melt together the butter and chocolate in a bowl over simmering water. Leave to cool, then mix with the almonds and crushed biscuits. Press down into the tin to form a base and pop into the fridge for 15 minutes or so.

3. Pre-heat the oven to 150°C (fan), 170°C, gas mark 3. With your electric whisk, beat the cream cheese, soured cream and sugar till light and fluffy. Add 4 of the eggs, one at a time. When combined, add the lime zest and juice. Mix.

4. Separately whisk 2 egg whites to soft peaks, then fold into the creamy mixture and combine. Pour over the base and bake for 1 hour, 20 minutes in the middle of the oven.

5. Leave to cool for 2–3 hours at room temperature, then pop into the fridge overnight.

Serve with pouring cream.

Break-your-diet brownies

If you only bake one thing in your entire life, let it be these. Grown men have begged me on their hands and knees for more . . . and they wanted a second brownie, too.

ALL YOU NEED IS

180g dark chocolate
180g butter
260g caster sugar
3 large eggs

80g plain flour
50g cocoa powder
200g Galaxy milk chocolate,
   roughly chopped

ALL YOU DO IS

1. Pre-heat your oven to 180°C (fan), 200°C, gas mark 6 and line a brownie tin with baking paper. (I use a 25 x 25cm ceramic dish that works well.) Let the paper fall over the edge so that you can use it to lift the cake out later.

2. Break up the dark chocolate and put it into a glass or metal bowl with the butter. Gently melt until smooth. Let it cool slightly.

3. Separately beat the sugar and eggs with an electric whisk until creamy, then fold into the chocolate mixture.

4. Sift the flour and cocoa over the whole lot and mix in with a big metal spoon.

5. Finally, fold in the chopped-up chocolate pieces. Pour into your dish and bake for 35–40 minutes.

6. Leave to cool before lifting out, using the lining paper as a sling. Cut into squares. The size is up to you. Mini bites for mini mouths and, frankly, huge slabs for me.

Serve warm (choc melting) with vanilla ice-cream.

'Good afternoon' apple cake

This cake has that wonderful 'Grandma made this' sort of a vibe. It reminds me of my grandma, Ivy. As a kid, I remember she marked every important occasion in my life with a cake. My birthday, my tooth falling out, my terrible exam results, and on and on. I think it's probably a blessing that she passed away before I lost my virginity . . . I miss her and her cakes.

ALL YOU NEED IS

150g soft butter
Don't forget: take the butter out of the fridge

150g golden caster sugar, plus 1 tablespoon to sprinkle

3 large eggs

1 teaspoon vanilla extract

120g plain or white spelt flour, sifted

80g ground almonds

1½ teaspoons baking powder

2 large eating apples, peeled and sliced

ALL YOU DO IS

1. Pre-heat your oven to 180°C (fan), 200°C, gas mark 6 and line your tin or dish. (I use a 20cm square ceramic oven dish, lined so I can lift out the cake using the paper, or a loose-bottomed cake tin around the same size.)

2. With an electric whisk, cream the butter and sugar until light and fluffy (don't stress too much).

3. Beat the eggs and vanilla, then add to the mixture a little at a time until well combined.

4. Separately mix the flour, almonds and baking powder. Then fold into the cake mix. Combine without over-mixing.

5. Pour and scrape into your tin or dish. Arrange the sliced apples gently on top and sprinkle with a tablespoon of golden caster sugar.

6. Bake for 45 minutes. Remove and leave to cool before removing from the tin.

Serve with a cup of tea and an open fire.

My mum's apple and blackberry crumble

This is a classic, comforting, easy everyday pudding. It's my mum's recipe, except that I have taken out most of the sugar and used sweet apples instead. Better for their teeth and my hips. My kids shout 'Grandma Crumbley!' whenever they see her. She thinks it's in reference to her skin but I'm sure it's her pudding.

ALL YOU NEED IS

500g sweet eating apples

300g blackberries

120g wholemeal or spelt flour

40g light brown sugar

30g ground almonds

100g butter, cubed

extra brown sugar for sprinkling

ALL YOU DO IS

1. Pre-heat the oven to 180°C (fan), 200°C, gas mark 6. Peel, core and slice the apples. Wash the berries.

2. Pop them all into a saucepan with a tablespoon of water and the lid on and cook over a medium heat for about 5–10 minutes, until they start to soften. Pour into an ovenproof ceramic dish.

3. For the crumble, mix the flour, sugar and almonds in a bowl and add the butter. With your fingertips, rub it all together to form a crumb-like texture.

4. Scatter the crumble mix over the fruit, then sprinkle some extra sugar on top of the whole lot. (I only use the extra sugar over half of the pie so the younger kids can tuck in without a dental drama.)

5. Bake for 40 minutes.

Serve with half-fat crème fraîche or vanilla ice-cream.

I love cold crumble for breakfast, but maybe that's just me . . .

Babies: *Hold back some cooked fruit and add to breakfast cereals or yogurt.*

I-promise-it's-easy pavlova

I had to include a pavlova as my husband, Dan, is an Aussie. I really do promise it will work. In fact, once you master it, it will be the pudding you are famous for. It's easy, looks great, you can make the base days in advance and everyone loves it. It's also fabulous as a birthday or celebration cake.

ALL YOU NEED IS

3 large egg whites

175g caster sugar

1 level teaspoon cornflour

1 teaspoon white vinegar

300ml whipping cream

1 tablespoon elderflower cordial

2 ripe mangoes

3 ripe passion fruit

ALL YOU DO IS

1. Pre-heat the oven to 150°C (fan), 170°C, gas mark 3 and line a baking sheet with baking paper.

2. With an electric whisk, whisk the egg whites until stiff, then whisk in the sugar a teaspoon at a time until very thick and glossy.

3. Mix the cornflour and vinegar together and whisk into the egg whites.

4. Spread the mixture in a circle about 8 inches in diameter (or shape of your choice) on the lined tray. Build up the edges a little so that they're higher than the middle.

5. Pop the meringue into the middle of the oven and bake for 1 hour. Leave it in the oven until completely cold or overnight. (DO NOT PEEK!)

6. Before serving, whisk the cream, then fold in the elderflower cordial. Pop it into the fridge until you are ready.

To serve, just pile the cream into the middle of the pavlova, scatter the mangoes and scrape the seeds of the passion fruit over the top.

Party jelly boats

Personally, I hate jelly. But a plate of these is such a pretty addition to your party table and it seems most little people will bare-knuckle fight to get their gnashers around some.

ALL YOU NEED IS

3 large oranges
135g pack fruit jelly
coloured tissue paper cut into sail shapes
12 cocktail sticks

ALL YOU DO IS

1. Cut the oranges in half across the middle and remove but keep the flesh. Try not to damage the shells.

2. Make up the jelly according to the packet instructions. You can use the reserved juice as part of the liquid. Chop the flesh from just one orange into little pieces.

3. Put the shells on a tray that fits in your fridge and fill them first with the chopped orange flesh, evenly distributed, then with the jelly mix. Pop into the fridge for an hour or so minimum (or overnight).

4. Once set, cut the oranges in half again. Put a sail on each stick and place in your jelly boat. All kids will want more than 1 boat, so allow for 2 each.

Tip: *Make these well in advance if you have room in your fridge.*

Kids' party planner

If you make just a couple of things yourself, it gives the appearance that you have made it all, if you know what I mean. Some fairy lights spread out on the table look great and my advice is stick to one colour for the balloons. It looks better and it avoids tears because so-and-so just got the last purple one.

1–6 years

DO THE DAY BEFORE

1. Cheat's jam tarts (p. 192).

2. Jelly boats (p. 242).

3. Sausage rolls (p. 52).
   (Put together. Cook on the day, then cut into bite-size pieces.)

4. Break-your-diet brownies (p. 234).
   (Bite-size, with a raspberry on top.)

DO ON THE DAY

1. Finger sandwiches. Invest in a fun-shaped biscuit cutter for these.

2. A plate of crudités. Cut up cucumber, carrot, tomatoes, celery, peppers, etc. and serve with a bowl of houmous.

3. A bowl of strawberries.

4. Cheese and apple on sticks.

5. Some grissini, cookies, crisps, a bowl of chocolate buttons or similar.

6. How about a bowl of ice lollies (p. 206) for pudding?

7. The cake, of course, and juice cartons.

Bosh!

6–60 years

KEEP IT SIMPLE

1. Some cut-up veg and a bowl of houmous.

2. Garlic bread (p. 145). (In soldiers.)

3. Tuna burgers (p. 167). (Stick a flag in them.)

4. Chips (p. 51). (Wrapped in little paper cones.)

5. Chocolate fondue (p. 197).

6. I-promise-it's-easy pavlova (p. 241).

7. Some jugs of drink (from juice to Pimm's).

Bish bosh!

Christmas list

There was a time when my Christmas list went a bit like this:

* sexy knickers
* trip to Paris
* day spa
* hangover cure . . .

Now it reads a bit like this:

Please, Santa, may I have:

* a Microplane grater
* a lemon zester
* a food processor
* an electric whisk
* a rice cooker
* a heavy-bottomed casserole pot
* some good Tupperware
* a sharp knife or two
* a couple of loose-bottomed cake tins
* a pair of tongs
* a magic whisk

You can still ask for the knickers, but this lot are invaluable. Beg, borrow or steal them if you must.

Plan B

You're having a bad day, you meant to stop and buy some sausages on the way home, but you ran into your ex, who had an eighteen-year-old on their arm and a new Jag, or your car got towed, with the dog in it, or you just plain forgot. Whatever . . .

. . . You need a Plan B.

Obviously you should already have the basics in your cupboard: eggs, flour, bread, sugar, oil, tins of tuna, etc., but start to stock up on some luxury items for days when you have to improvise.

STUFF TO HAVE IN THE LARDER

* runny honey
* balsamic vinegar
* toasted flaked almonds
* ground almonds
* plain cashew nuts
* pine nuts
* porridge oats
* dark chocolate
* cocoa powder
* cornflakes
* dried chilli flakes
* good-quality pesto
* Dijon mustard
* tin of olives (green, stuffed with anchovies, are tops)
* sun-blushed tomatoes

STUFF TO HAVE IN THE FRIDGE

* half-fat crème fraîche
* lemons
* lardons or pancetta
* black lumpfish caviar
* some goat's cheese

STUFF FOR THE FREEZER

* fresh herbs (just freeze, then crush with your hands when needed)
* fresh ginger (so much easier to grate from frozen)
* vanilla ice-cream
* frozen berries

Index

Acknowledgements

I have loved every minute of this and want to say thanks to:

* My kids and my Dan for eating the burnt bits.

* My darling friend Neris for the introduction, the soup and her extraordinary energy and encouragement.

* Amanda, for trying (please don't stop).

* Lindsey. Your patience and support have been humbling.

* David and your gang. God knows you were hen-pecked, but I love these photos.

* Mima, Beth and Margie. Your washing-up, chopping and cups of tea were the backbone of the shoot.

* Paul, for not just laughing at me and telling me to go home and get an acting job.

* Vicky, for joining in and cooking my food, my way, for my kids.

* Bob for his bird and Jonty for making it clear when things got too buttery.

* Trish for advice and tips from the mountain.

* Sarah F, Sarah W, Sarah R and Sarah H. It looks like a proper book, how did you do that?

* M&S: we love your pants.

* Everyone at Penguin for giving a damn.

* Michael, Carlos and Maria, who against all the odds made me look half decent.

* So many thanks to Mum, Briggette, Marion, John, Amy, Jeanie, Jenny, Zoe, Emma, Pants and Dix.

* And very importantly to Bren. You are the woman I wish I was . . .

Thank you all. x

my family, By Parker